UNKNOWN PATHWAYS

PAUL ZEPPELIN

UNKNOWN PATHWAYS

iUniverse books may be ordered through booksellers or by contacting:

iUniverse
1663 Liberty Drive
Bloomington, IN 47403
www.iuniverse.com
1-800-Authors (1-800-288-4677)

ISBN: 978-1-6632-0486-8 (sc)
ISBN: 978-1-6632-0487-5 (e)

Library of Congress Control Number: 2020912980

Print information available on the last page.

iUniverse rev. date: 07/15/2020

Preface for *Unknown Pathways*

This is the third volume of poetry by Paul Zeppelin following *Shattered Silence* and *Naked Trees.* Paul writes ever inventive enigmatic yet often intimate and sensual poems. His sometimes controversial, provocative but philosophically justified views are expressed laconically with an effortless flow of musically rhythmical phrases. Paul's verse is like a morning breeze of fresh air, which is badly needed in today's poetic efforts that deviate from the poetic genre. The poetry contains attractive thoughts and his allegories and symbolism take central stage and capture the imagination.

    I highly recommend this book of lyricism, wit and a veiled heartfelt storytelling.

Judith Parrish Broadbent
Author of *Golden Days:
Stories and Poems of the
Middle South and Beyond.*

Unknown pathways lead to a well known world

Contents

Anew

I am a disillusioned dork:
I need to ask my mother
About that thoughtless stork
That dumped me at her door
Yet was aware of my good father.
He better get ready for a real war.

Dark clouds steadily roll in,
Rain doused the sunset's flames,
My glands made more adrenalin,
So, I can figure out newer blames.

Five races started by the primal word
Black, brown, yellow, red and white
Make love in every corner of the world,
Adjusting our order with their might,
Aiming much farther, higher, faster,
Deleting olden rules of our quagmire,
And spreading our imminent disaster.

They make some ripples in the pools
That rock their boring years ahead,
As passengers on the ship of fools,
They only waste their daily bread.

My toes already test the waters,
Yet I still meander in the blew,
And say, "Lets flip the quarters,
And recreate the world anew."

Our Foolish World

It is our foolish world:
We burn the bridges
Between our sorrows;
Just mark my word,
We will destroy all sieges,
We will embrace tomorrows

We navigate our lives' ocean,
Not all is fish that's in the net;
Sometimes the efforts of a fairy
Set our perceptions into motion,
Perhaps, not quite sufficient,
But doubtlessly necessary.

We rush back home we love,
We run from daily stresses,
We want these days to end,
We think, we've had enough;
The night is ready to descend
If she remembers our addresses.

We argue, fist our hands,
We leave and shut the doors,
We walk away aloneness' bound,
We still wear our wedding bands,
Our hearts bleed onto the floors,
Our screams don't make a sound.

The memories of bitter tears,
Like silhouettes of sprinters
Run from the sunny springs
Toward their freezing years;

The real diamonds of winters,
Unknown to the wedding rings.

The Cruelty of Life

I squandered many years,
Under Saint Peter's Dome,
My tired conscience veers
Away from ancient Rome.

The world is not about faith,
It is about artificial power:
We are revolving in a lathe,
And waiting for a happy hour.

I quaff my luscious wine,
I cheat on useless rules;
Our roots are not divine,
We live among the mules.

Looks matter to the mind,
Mean nothing to the blind.

Who are these people?
Who are these strangers?
Only a shallow rolling ripple
Of never-ending dangers.

The cruelty of life,
Is like a rhapsody in gray,
And yet, I learned to thrive
In premonition of another day.

Cosmic Dust

I am wiping cosmic dust,
Infinity already crumbles,
Our galaxy's blind trust
Flip-flops and fumbles.

I'll change my mind
When so-called facts
Will veer their kind
Into the fertile tracts.

I followed David's glance
Before the pebble's throw:
Goliath had a chance
To dodge the fatal blow.

History died that day,
History freed the past,
Mystery strode away,
To have a life, at last.

I hope you heard,
I am a decent singer,
Almost a mockingbird;
Be simply my girlfriend,
I have no finger
For a wedding band.

Slide out of your dress,
Undo your golden hair,
I am so eager to caress
The wreck of our affair.

I raked the tiny beads of my devoured youth,
The history repeats to hurt--never to soothe.

The Crescent Learns to Fly

My angel hovers in the sky,
The stars shine on his face;
The crescent learns to fly
Before the sun's embrace.

We tango to the end of night,
I kiss blue sadness of her eyes;
Hopes drown in the melting ice,
Love has no future in plain sight.

We graduated from the night;
New dawn smears our tears,
Our love fades into the light,
Into the heartless crowd's jeers.

And only my subconscious
Whispers, "Spring is upon us:
The seeds of cherries
Are waiting in the frozen ground,
And very soon, the berry-fairies
Will show off their taste around."

The End of an Endless Sky

I walked my extra mile,
I stood against the Wailing Wall,
Behaving like a mute bystander.
I knew, God leaves us in a while
As if he has decided to surrender
Foreseeing our endless downfall.

I tightly closed my eyes,
He didn't touch my face,
I saw a magic of his rise,
But didn't seek his grace.

I wished to see the road ahead,
The persevering good and bad,
I wanted to have wings and fly
Into the end of an endless sky.

I trust, the winds will blow,
I trust, the trees will sway,
The river-time will flow,
And wash my sins away.

Farewell. My universe capsized:
Gods judge; the mortals save.
I reached the end and realized,
We'll be equal only in the grave.

My Critics' Guillotine

My ancient table lamp was lit,
I wrote a verse and marveled,
Then rearranged it bit by bit;
The road well traveled.

Right at the end of my nightshift.
I ask my muse, "What I possess?'
"Neither a big talent, nor a tiny gift,"
That's what she always says.

A cozy comfort of my morning,
It is not dull and never boring,
It is my daily fruitful routine,
Beyond my critics' guillotine.

They see no forest
For the trees,
They see no florist
For the bees.

These oracles of knowledge
Didn't descend from bliss,
These troubadours of carnage
Ascend from the abyss,
And put a stick into my spokes,
For them I am just a hoax.

I am like an actor in silent films:
I cry, nobody hears,
I talk, nobody listens.
Sometimes I change my gears,
But I am still the same,
No money and no fame.

The City Chaos is in Order

Life-juror disregards my valor,
A verdict is in black and white,
A rainbow lost its yellow color,
A raven-cloud blocks the light.

I play my old accordion,
You listen to my stuff,
The show goes on,
It is my one-way love.

The city chaos is in order,
Even the mess of Broadway;
I gather thoughts and solder
A bridge into the Milky Way.

We drift apart,
I am on the way
To get our drinks;
Your iceberg-heart
Will melt one day
While wisdom blinks.

The scent of pumpkin bread,
The sound of a falling apple,
Those days are quickly fled.
I dust my moth-eaten uniform
To fight another useless storm,
Only the bloody sabers rattle.

My merciless death
Was never crowned,
I held my final breath,
I truly was love-bound.

I will be back,
War isn't the end of lives,
I will be back,
If our tired love survives,
I will be back
Before our stars are fallen,
I will be back
Before your heart is stolen,
I will be back,
Only the dead,
Have seen the end.

The Eve of a New Year

Some crawl, the others fly;
Life-teacher is quite stern,
I read the books and learn
To eat and have the pie.

Gods won't forgive,
They need the guilty;
Those who just take
But never try to give.
Only the fallen angel
Admires the thrifty.

The rosy petals lying in the dust
Like teardrops of strong men,
I didn't earn my angel's trust,
He left; I didn't notice when.

Euphoria and trepidation:
The eve of a New Year,
Farewell to what was dear;
I am in the midst of cheers,
I walk across jubilation,
But close my eyes,
To hide my tears.

The Enigmatic Doorway

The future is devouring itself,
The wars kidnapped our lives,
Even a hallow portrait of myself
Was varnished with my lies.

The enigmatic doorway
Hid images of badness;
A dying candle on the tray
Lit the oblivion of sadness.

My books snooze on the shelves,
My comic tragedies about love:
Banalities unleashed themselves,
But didn't bring us close enough.

I never learned to fly, I crawl
Under the arches of a rainbow;
I barely know anything at all
Beyond my first stone's throw.

The muddy river of my verses
Runs towards poetic carnage,
Towards my critics' daily curses,
Under a futile tree of knowledge.

Obituary Was Never Printed

A pair of steadfast guards
Peter and Paul could wait,
I whistled past graveyards
In front of that elusive gate.

The clouds took my feelings to the gods,
I hung on ropes like boxers in the ring,
I only asked myself, "What are the odds
For me to live and see another spring?"

I craved to see my fragile paradise,
I craved to justify my premonition,
I craved to see with my own eyes
The promised bliss or yet another
Egotistical ambition.

My life marched toe-to-toe
With Matthew's daily prayer,
There was a "quid pro quo"
With my Lord's son and heir.
He always welcomed changes,
He didn't let me suffer in today,
He sent a pair of angels
To walk with mops and buckets
Across my yesterdays.

Horses got out of the stables,
The fish jumped out of the water,
The moon hung on the gables,
My soul escaped the slaughter.

Life was so brief, I died last night,
There is no grief, there is no light;
My life-train didn't leave the station,
Heaven upholds the same location;

Nobody's fault, no one has failed,
It is my life that silently derailed...

Obituary was never printed
By a newspaper no-one-reads,
My death was never even hinted
In articles of properties proceeds.

The Sun Still Rises

The moon lights edges of the clouds,
They hang like sloppy patches
On the familiar, tattered night;
It is the time to make my rounds
Along the bars with rusty latches
And hug the barflies of limelight.

Somewhere, above the clouds
Our souls may meet again.
We dumped our bloody shrouds,
And angels saw our scars of pain.

Each one of us has plenty to regret,
We cannot sleep; the sun still rises,
We all are burdened with the debt
Owed to life's unfortunate surprises.

We stroll a trembling lifelong bridge
Between the tyranny and privilege,
Between the beautiful and ugly,
Between the beer and bubbly,
Between the good and evil,
Between the pointer and retriever,
Between the strong and feeble,
Between the order and upheaval.

We humbly hope,
Somewhere between the clouds
Ascend our souls and fall our shrouds.

The Guilt of Theft

I walked away alone
And to the right,
You also went alone,
But to the left;
Lights were too bright
Above my guilt of theft.

I think about you,
When I am kissing others,
I think about you,
When conscience bothers,
I think about you,
When I am on the brink,
I think about you,
When sinking in my drink.

…

The Chosen Few

The yellow David's stars
Gilded the nightly skies;
I saw the lifelong scars
In darkness of her eyes.

The chosen few,
Possessors of the old,
Inventors of the new,
Required to be bold,
Forced to defend
Their precious lives,
Their Promised Land
In their eternal strives.

Life hovers like a gull,
Above their endless fear,
Under the blinding sun;
A brush of Mark Chagall
Tells everyone,
The end is not yet near.

Life plays the strings
Of falling, sloping rain;
Only a rainbow brings
New hopes past pain.

I Slid from Greatness

The waterfalls of tears are dry,
I slid from greatness to the floor,
My world turned upside down,
I am an angel fallen from the sky,
I am just a shadow at the door,
I am a contour of a tragic clown.

While my originality is dying,
The blind still lead the blind.
I failed to write a single verse
Without suffering and crying.
My weary and frustrated mind
Is trying to dismiss this curse.

What else is new, I am a sinner,
My tiny list of Christmas cards
Appears unquestionably thinner,
I'll keep my lever in reverse,
My friends won't get regards,
Won't read my heartfelt verse.

At times, they'll hear my name,
I shamelessly enjoy its fame.
I am a pupil of Sigmund Freud,
I am spear fishing in my quests
To entertain the brightest minds,
I am evading silence of the void,
But judge the value of my finds,
Amongst the uninvited guests.

The stars still vainly blinking,
Lives hang on the edge of night,
Utopias are quickly sinking
Into the tempting morning light.

I am a passing silhouette of war,
I leave no footprints on the floor.

I Play Only the Melody I Know

I am an actor on a life's stage,
I wear a mask of silent rage,
A looming social apocalypse
Brings only chains and whips.

The church's bells don't ring,
The wingless birds don't sing,
The fallen angels failed to find
The deaf, the numb, the blind.

The piles of gold and silver
Will lose their precious glow,
I am a humble country fiddler,
I play only the melody I know.

I try to hide my grace or attitude,
I wouldn't flaunt my joy or grief,
I am a lonely beacon on the cliff,
I am writing poetry of solitude.

She Chirped a Pretty Fable

She chirped a pretty fable to my ear,
I tenderly caressed her lovely face,
I drowned in her eyes without fear,
I sensed Chanel, but just a trace...

The full moon floated at the gable
Wrapped in the quilt of starry skies;
Two candles cried on our coffee table,
It was the final night for our goodbyes.

If loving her was wrong,
Why didn't she talk to me?
She never let me sing my song,
And yet I thought I dwell in glee.

This vaudeville is dead,
Don't ever mourn,
Don't cry at its deathbed,
I am free at last. I am airborne.

I swigged my "Maker's Mark"
Then soared into a better place,
Where nights are short and dark,
But long and sunny are the days.

I didn't have to walk too far
To break-in my shiny shoes,
The happy strings of my guitar
Didn't yet learn to play the blues.

I lost the scent of her perfume,
Forgot the color of her eyes,
New daffodils already bloom
Under the springtime 's melting ice.

Scherzo

Life's knocking on my door
Anticipating rite of spring.
I peeled my shadow off the floor
And soared into the blue to sing.

I passed the devil on the left,
God passed me on the right,
I was quite young and deft,
No one could stop my flight.

Although, Good Friday passed,
Jesus has died but resurrected
To care for chosen and elected.
A shocking evidence was raked
As a sweet memo from the past,
"Orgasms of history were faked."

Bright Easter and Passover gone,
Lackluster days are here to stay,
Only the sparrows chirp at dawn
Expecting yet another sunny day.

Provence

The land of a guilty joy,
I am your albatross,
I have returned;
Provence.
The most delicious ploy,
The bridges crossed,
The bridges burned,
At once.

Provence,
The moons passed by,
You haven't aged a day.
Provence,
Only my hair is fully gray,
A sign of a long goodbye.

Provence,
I am a two-fisted drinker
Of a single barrel scotch;
Provence,
Pour me a happy sinker,
Let's go up a notch.

My only fighting chance,
Mon Sud de la France,
So long all pros and cons,
Hello, my love, Provence.

Poesy

I write with hope never to fail
To carve those words I know,
Along the footprints on a trail,
Over the virgin shawl of snow.

My muse writes songs and sings,
I put them on the piece of paper
Into a poem with a pair of wings
But send it to the sky much later.

I wandered as an aimless cruise
Which navigates across a maze;
The sunshine brought my muse
So stunning, I could only gaze.

I send away the thoughts I write
Somewhere into the starry night,
And dance across my fussy lines
Between the futile warning signs.

My verses climb onto the pages,
Drag feet amid the thirsty verbs,
Fly over the senseless hedges
Into the wreath of fragrant herbs.

The tangled flesh of every noun
Nibbled and savored by my pen,
Yet rather vague to be devoured,
But full of flavor as a perfect ten.

She was My Magic Curse

The joy of weddings,
The shyly lifted gowns,
The virgin silky beddings
Under the golden crowns.

I learned new tongues
Sailing the foreign seas,
I heard her parting songs
Before our marriage-freeze.

Sang with a naughty flare
Over the land of our affair.

She was my tiny albatross
She was my magic curse,
She was my heavy cross,
She was my caring nurse,
She was my passion play,
She was a predator,
I was a willing prey.

Sheet Music in the Sky

The jolly birds sit on the wires,
A great sheet music in the sky,
They sing, my tiny happy flyers;
A nasty winter pledged goodbye.

Long live the rite of spring,
Long live a lifetime trend:
The merry birds will always sing
Their songs with the happy end.

All of a sudden,
Rain torn the sky in stripes
With its slanted crystal strings;
The sun abruptly disappeared
Behind the clouds;
Cowardly hid its rays,
And waited for the winds
To rise above the idle crowds,
To tear the leaded clouds,
And free the sunny beams.

A rainbow bent
As if it were a Triumph arc
Commemorating happiness,
A God sent genuine landmark.

Rachmaninoff-Piano Concerto No. 2

You are in every breath,
You are so close to birth,
You are so far from death,
You are eternally on Earth.

Rachmaninoff-Piano Concerto No. 2,
The harmonies of love and joy in play,
Dawn brings the tears of morning dew
From heaven's gates into my hazy day.

With you, I never have enough,
I climb the hues of rainbow arc,
To hear your melodies of love,
Without them it's cold and stark.

The flow of a sun-wrapped sound
Brings glee to every soul around,
Your piano is the all-forgiving love
And Eric Carmen hums from above:
"When making love
Was just for fun,
Those days have gone…"

We live, our minds still learn,
Amazing music still caresses
Our dreams of hope and glee;
The stars of elegance still burn,
Only Rachmaninoff still wrestles,
Only his harmonies will set us free.

Nike Has a Single Wing

We knew our victory isn't on the track,
The plans for our defeat are stacked,
We march in silence, birds don't sing,
Even a goddess Nike has a single wing.

The tears of melancholy write my lyrics,
Courageous warriors perish in the dusk,
Our rare victories are continually Pyrrhic,
The bitter seeds of doubt drop their husk.

It was a merciless acidic farce
Of a bloody warmonger Mars;
Our destiny sent a nasty treat,
We traded victory for a defeat.

So cold, the birds are leaving,
It is a sign of our dreary fate,
The saints are sadly grieving,
Forgiveness comes too late.

Nobody Comes to See my Grave

I teased my fate,
I walked tightropes
Above the isles of hate.
Under the skies of hopes,
I sold my soul and mind,
To prophets of the blind.

Nobody comes to see my grave
Under a weeping willow's wings,
It is much cooler in the shade,
But every now and then, I wave
To a brave nightingale that sings,
A tiny bird who is absolutely free,
Obsessed with her sparkling glee.
I learned the melodies she played,
Her music took me to the world
I've never dreamt or seen before,
St. George unsheathed his sword
And led me to a sacramental door.

Openly lecherous worn-out girls
Caress my misery and loneliness
Yet I am drinking in the half-lit bars,
Where loudly inviting music swirls
Above the endless uselessness
Of our faith into the falling stars.

Only a few last yards
Into a secret haven
Where bogus bards
Or a ferocious raven

Guarding the red sunrise,
A curtain hiding daily lies.

Wide-eyed,
I went inside.

Reluctant Blessing

Unneeded
And reluctant blessing
Descended from the sky;
Unheeded
As a bitter dressing
Over the apple pie.

I am in the belly of the whale,
Job was a saint, but I may fail
To worship, hope and wait,
And drown in despair of hate.

I am not looking for a ford
To cross the feisty creek
Or all devouring quagmire.
Life-mother cut the cord,
I am too old and weak
To hate or to admire.

First love, your kiss
Left sugar on my lips;
The only mindful truth
In games of our youth.

False condemnations
Scarred my soul,
The stones were thrown
At my flesh;
I can't relearn my daily role,
I can't restart my life afresh.

Reluctant blessing
Descended from the sky,
Too late; I said goodbye.

Shattered Monoliths

I cannot play a game of poker,
My face is calmly legible to all,
I hate to be somebody's prey;
I'd rather be a vapid joker
Than walking ten feet tall
As a role model on feet of clay.

I claw across established myths
In search of irony in mordant wit,
In search of shattered monoliths,
In search of smaller shoes to fit.

Instead, I found ancient
Legends wrapped in lies,
That had a penchant
For blarney in disguise.

I entertain my scientific nihilism
By forcing rays of god sent light
Throughout a transparent prism.
It morphs the rays in seven sins;
Those seven sins of evil's show,
In seven arcs of a bright rainbow,
Welcomes the future to the night.
My theater ends. Reality begins.

.

Remaining Moons

I lived with hopes to be a poet;
Friends wished it wouldn't last,
My mother knew I'd outgrow it.
It was a dream. It was my past.

I am wasting my remaining moons,
Collecting foes instead of friends,
They are just country fair balloons
Or rather stocks without dividends.

I stanchly stick to my beliefs,
To my old-fashioned songs,
I even tried to shed bright lights
On ancient gloomy bas-reliefs,
On memories of golden wrongs
And myths about useless rights.

I am a priest who reprimands
Innocent virgins never kissed.
I traveled through the lands
That don't exist,
I pumped the brakes
And dropped a second shoe,
The swirling snowflakes
Covered the only path I knew.

I even tossed gold-laden invitations
From my decisive moneyed friends,
Those vanity caressing applications
Of means safeguarded by the ends

I dreamed to be a poet
But couldn't outgrow it.

Red Dancers

Who is that artist who paints your face?
Who is that brightest talent in the race?
He runs the corridor of glory and decay,
He guards the doors into a sinless day.

I bet it can be only you, Henri Matisse,
The best amid a few who painted bliss.

Life searches for the answers
Among the axioms and doubts,
Among the truths and chances,
Among the floods and droughts,
Among the wise and senseless,
Among the solitude and crowds.

Unknown to the cliquish sensors,
Hiding behind the useless fences
Dividing vulnerable modern arts,
Only Matisse reveals the answers
To our minds, souls, and hearts
Through red Matisse's dancers.

Pirate's Limerick

I know Billy Bones
A one-eyed pirate,
A one-legged soul
With kidney stones.
He isn't mute or silent,
But he is out of control.

His loot is hidden,
He smokes the weed,
His will is badly written,
Nobody wants to read.

In our heartless world,
Somebody stole his peg,
He doesn't have a ride;
He cannot hear a word,
His famous parrot died,
Yet hatched a golden egg.

Today, he's not a player,
He doesn't drink his gin,
He rarely says a prayer,
Nor he commits a sin.

Among the chosen few,
He tries to end this life,
He is the only pirate Jew,
Who never lost a strife.

He gulped a keg of beer
Then dove into the ocean,
He overwhelmed his fear,
The sea is always kosher.

Please, Stop the Planet

Life was a one-way ticket,
Along the rails into nowhere,
Too strange and wicked,
But flashy as a country fair.

What have I done,
Where have I failed,
Where have you gone,
Which train have I derailed?

Why are you always
On the other side
Of our dining table?
You flaunt your gloomy face
As if someone already died
In my so far unwritten fable.

I spent my life to plan it,
I beg you on my knees,
Please, stop the planet,
I'll step down to the sky
And I'll grow wings to fly
Above the naked trees.

Life plays the game of shells
Within two crossing parallels;
Along my yet unwritten lines.

I am aware. I read the signs.

Normandy

The winds of war painted the sky in red,
The drums of war were dire and loud,
The dark and heavy, leaded cloud
Was the last blanket of the dead,
For them it was the final war...
I see a new one at the door.

War is too brutal with the brave,
I see a somber dusty cross
On my abandoned grave;
It is the Croix de Guerre
For which I died in flare.
The one I truly earned.

The bridge is futile
When it's burned.

Only the Bridge was Burned

I am forever trying to arrange
My verses as a sweet revenge,
For my somewhat dejected past,
For worried memories that last,
For thank you notes unsent,
For pain that came and went,
For long sunsets of a dying love,
For every push that came to shove.

The circumstances of my death
Invented glory of my final breath;
My plodding but infuriating life
Insisted on a comfortable end;
A spectacle which must pretend
That past was a slowly falling knife.

I heard the wartime drums,
I lost my own creative voice,
I had no choice,
I left being upset and grieving;
I learned redemption rarely comes
To people virtuous but unforgiving.

I left behind two sins,
My vanity and pride;
Annoying twins
Enjoying a free ride.

But then, I changed my mind,
I have returned,
The sentence wasn't signed,
Only the bridge was burned

Life-Carousel Still Moves

Life-carousel still moves,
The horses smoothly run,
We hear the noisy hooves
Under the scorching sun.

We drink to run our hearts,
We quickly learn the arts
Of living on the edge,
But keeping our pledge
Not to wind up in paradise,
But to escape a bloody hell.
The sun will always rise
Above our church's bell.

We are motorcycle-borne,
Beer canned in our throats,
Our manhood tries to learn
To navigate its daily thoughts
Toward our barefaced desires
Away from promised paradise.

We leave our youth,
We leave our cozy nest,
We never learn the truth,
We never learn the best

The remnants of our genesis survived,
The views we keep in emphasis revived,
Ideas of our nation's founders obscured,
Their fears of our future won't be cured.

She Wanted Me to Walk

I fly under the quilt of clouds
Through snow, rain and hail,
I am a hawk over the crowds,
I am a guard of the Holy Grail.

She whispered with her honey lips
The words of love,
Then bowled like throw of the dice,
And aired her useless, wicked kiss.
My days are wrapped in silent cries,
I've had enough.

I had a morbid whim:
They dressed me up and raved,
They laid me on my deathly bed,
My road to heaven wasn't paved,
Few cried, most wanted to forget,
The scene was grim.
They tossed the earthly ambers
Into my grave to please my fate.
Those days, no one remembers,
I hovered far away; I couldn't wait.

She wanted me to walk,
But I am soaring to the sky,
I am not a dove; I am a hawk,
From now on, I will forever fly.

Paul Sent You

I am a dead cat bounce,
Why do you bother me?
I am not inspired anymore.
Don't ask me to denounce
A year of peace and glee
And write about bloody war.

Even the dead take flights
Into the Promised Land,
Consuming their birthrights
Received first hand.

Even the darkest corner
May have a sunny window,
I looked at every mourner
And saw my smiling widow:
She wouldn't drop a single
Tear,
My angel whispered in her
Ear,
"When you'll meet
Someone in hell,
Be honest, be discreet,
Just say, Paul sent you.
To them you're a raw meat,
Your face won't ring the bell,
Don't march to your own beat,
Just say, Paul sent you."

At times, life was so rough,
I could no longer bear,
And muttered "C'est la Guerre."
Today, I am dead, but tough,
I fly above the fields of glee,
And whisper "C'est la Vie."

Since God's Been Gone

Since God's been gone,
Our existence after death
Excludes both pro and con:
No bliss, only a final breath.

The demons and the gods,
The blind amid the artists,
The atheists and Baptists
Fused by the lightning rods.

I sip from a Sunday chalice,
I play my requiem on a violin,
A genuine apostasy of malice,
My homage to Mary Magdalene.

Sincere apologies were begged,
Pity and clemency were earned,
Those bishops were four-legged,
Even her scrolls were burned.

I am watching burning candles
On the dining table;
Their trembling flames
Whisper a captivating fable
About arguments and scandals,
About wars and other games,
The wicked humans like to play
Until their heads no longer sway.

The Last, the parting Supper
Took place in the Upper Room,
It wasn't only gloom and doom:
The twelve received His body,
The twelve received His blood,
They tried His wine and bread.

He mentioned that somebody
Betrayed Him for a silver mud.
He will discuss it with his Dad.

I write this story from my tomb,
St. Luke is my Nom de Plume.

Six Strings of My Guitar

Six strings of my guitar,
Six comfy foreign tongues,
Six angels from afar,
Six rights, six wrongs,
I play in Paris; topless bar,
My angels wearing thongs.

Six came to fly,
But chose to walk,
Six came to cry,
But chose to talk.

Some come to cry and niggle,
Some come to pull the trigger,
Some learn what money is,
Some crave to hit, but miss.

I play my music every night,
The men are rude and loud,
They argue, drink and fight,
Just lonely, vain and proud.

The waves of darkness,
The rolling tides of truth,
So sweet, but heartless,
My river of eternal youth.

Pont Neuf over the Seine,
Are you all right? Très bien.
Six feet all underground;
Somebody lost; I found.

The staircase of vices,
I wonder what's on top,
Wine, food, sex, prices,
Or silence if I ever stop.

Pedantic Metronome

Pedantic metronome
Of our lives' highways
Moves shiny chrome
Along lackluster days.

Be smart, stay idle,
The Satan often wins,
Don't trust your idol,
Enjoy your seven sins.

Even the newest door
Hangs on shrill hinges,
Don't dive into the war,
Enjoy the quiet fringes.

Stay with the sinners,
Wolf down sour wine,
The minus is the plus;
We are the winners,
Don't cross that line,
The foe is never us.

I Have to Choose

I have to choose
Between two moons,
One swims across the sky,
Another drowns in the lake,
One flies too high,
Another is a mirrored fake.

I have to choose
Between two moons,
One's rocking on the waves,
Another is above and wanes,
A tarnished silver in my sight,
A glinting lantern in the flight.

I have to choose
Between two moons,
A bird above the land
Is worse than one in hand,
I chose the floating fake,
Because I own that lake.

My Efforts Died in Vain

I walk the corridors of power,
I cross this torturous terrain,
Even the apples grow sour
Under the downhearted rain.

The last chance weakens,
I am a giant with clay legs:
I put my bets on chickens
Against the golden eggs.

My boat is docked,
My life has failed,
My room is locked,
My soul is jailed.

I calculated all the odds:
And yet my willful blindness
Forgot the arrogance of gods
And used my sinful kindness.

I always close my eyes
To see the whirling dice;
I asked my angel-savior
To spin them to my favor.

I missed a happy hour,
My efforts died in vain.

I Tried to Be a Saint

It was entirely clear:
I tried to be a saint,
I didn't lie or steal,
I didn't fall or faint.

The saints don't ever sleep,
Their tears wash our faith,
They pray for us and weep
Till sins will learn to bathe.

I am a nervous wreck
I am a shuffled deck,
I am back on Earth,
It is my place of birth.

I gathered every bit of power,
The gods allowed me to earn;
It was my sacramental hour,
But yet, I chose the downturn.

It was from the horse's mouth:
Hell is for the moody North,
Bliss is for the happy South;
I really knew what it is worth:
The former was much better,
Nevertheless, I took the latter.

Some say I waste my life
Of which I am an owner;
They want a smoky dive,
I long for a quiet corner.

I followed Jesus for awhile,
I even walked an extra mile

Under the yoke of burdens.
Today, I am a mighty truck
That clears religious hurdles
And wishes y'all good luck.

Stars Fade and Die

The stars don't outlive
The sinners anymore,
We are squarely even;
They faint and leave,
No hope for an encore.
Forgotten and forgiven.

Stars fade and die,
And shyly disappear
Into the leaded sky;
I let my angel sing
First far then near,
While bells still ring

I see their flying souls,
Good things end well,
Stars left black holes
Then yelled," farewell!"
It was the sacred word
Which started our world.

Revolving Doors

I early realized I am the best
Amid all fighters in the ring,
I fight for peace and rest
Till a fat lady starts to sing.
Although these days I hear,
"Your soul is yet unsaved,
Before you climb up here,
Your road must be paved."

Another stolen night
From altars of delight,
I desperately veer
From dusk until sunrise,
Across the teary fear
In your disappointed eyes.

It is a bloodless science
Of endless bloody wars:
The sadness of farewells
Brings gloss to our haloes,
Then ignorance of violence
Spins the revolving doors
From courts to prison cells
And back to our sinful laws.

I mix the lion's petrifying roar
With leaves from a naked tree
And clothe that naked emperor
Who lost the Holy Grail of glee.

My mind makes sentences
From tiny bits of precious gold
And sends them to my verses
Obscured by false pretenses.

Red Berries on a Perky Holly

Red berries on a perky holly
Lit by the Christmas beams,
The cloud of my melancholy
Handcuffs my daily dreams
About every sad teardrop,
About wars that never stop.

My thirst seems endless,
I drink and dream a lot
Along the piercing rains
Pleasing the devil's plot,
About a noisy madness
Of passing days and trains,
About their nervous wheels,
About a cacophony of rails,
About our harming deals
Beyond the cozy fairy tales.

I learn the misery of being blind,
I cannot heal my littered mind,
I cannot see the rays of dawn.
I see my buddies, who are gone;
They wander through a maze,
Close to the infinity of grace.

The Fertile Pasture of My Youth

Where is my youth along a fertile pasture?
Where is that blissful and dreamy place?
Where is the bird of hope I tried to capture?
Where is the garden of my innocence?

Where are the days of common sense?
Where are the guards of youth or friends?
Where are the roses, where are the thorns?
Where are the kings to occupy the thrones?

Where is the splendor a gliding swan?
Where is my granny's lily pond?
Where is the blinding, smiling sun?
Where is the monolith of our bond?

First date, first kiss, the first love ever,
I left behind those fading days forever,
I left the slimy moat of tears and pain,
I left the quagmires of greed and gain.

The malachite of grass is luminous but coy,
A nervous butterfly swirls like an autumn leaf,
Her wings are trembling with impatient joy,
Her happiness is timeless, her agony is brief.

I miss the doubts of my grief-stricken soul,
The stronghold of my curiosity was blown,
I walk the enigmatic path towards my goal,
I walk across the past towards the known.

The Fault is Mine Alone

We fought, you cried,
Our love came to an end,
The longest farewell night,
I fell apart; you didn't bend.

Our lives are squares of chessboards,
The prison cells for queens and kings,
The knights kill bishops with the swords,
The players fight and pull the strings.

Life is a stage; life is a theatre
That drowns in a blinding light,
A victory is sweet, defeat is bitter,
Like hurricanes after a quiet night.

I cannot outwit the Lord,
The fault is mine alone,
The only argument I can afford,
A loser shouldn't cast a stone.

The Fallen Try to Rise

The tender hearts of friends,
The glossy wedding bands,
Retain the memories of me,
I pay the price for being free,
The past is tightly closed,
I ramble as an aimless ghost.

I mask and veil my face,
I am a spirit in disguise,
I walk across the maze,
I see the fallen try to rise.

Beasts run the fields,
Birds pierce the air;
The future yields
For those who dare.

Old branches lash the clouds,
White cotton hid away the sky,
The tiny twigs as lacy shrouds
Wrapped those who cannot fly.

Two Silky Threads

The rails look like two silky threads
Intriguing, shiny, long and straight;
I hope this railroad never ends,
I hide my future in its freight.

It is the main road of my quest;
I took the worst, I took the best,
Even a bag with marvels of my soul,
This is my only life; it is my title role.

My daring life is like a terrifying film
That runs the past before my eyes:
Some happy years, some very grim,
Fiascos, wins, some truths and lies.

I grieve my buddies; they were the best,
A blanket of the night falls on my chest,
I clinch my teeth; my eyes refuse to cry.
I used to know every soul that went to fly.

It doesn't come as a surprise,
The sun will also rise.

The Graves I Never Dug

I search the rubbles
Of graves I never dug,
And hide the troubles,
I swept under the rug.

My angel never spoke
To my direct ancestors,
Those heavy boozers
That vanished broke;
Unfortunate investors,
Accomplished losers.

My tired shadow hides
In whispers of the trees
Like bright exotic birds,
Like first-kissed brides
Performing a striptease
For legally blind hordes.

The wingless angel,
The prince of fighting,
That vicious stranger
Removed my pledges,
Destroyed my writing,
Burned all the pages.

Life doesn't ever end
Like a nostalgic song,
Like a forgotten verse,
Or like a useless trend.
I simply said, "So long,
Farewell my universe."

I wonder if I will be unfit
For crazy predecessors,
I bet they fell into the pit
For obstinate aggressors.

While I am Still a Man

The heartless sober clouds
Buried the vodka-drunken sun;
It is too late for thank you bouts,
I tossed a hotdog on a bun.

A red haired young bartender,
Wearing a dusty military gear,
She is a boozer and offender
And pours me Guinness beer.

A trendy purple dotty polish
Shows off her hawkish nails;
She's serving sex as garnish
When every other effort fails.

My endless leisure
Rhymes with seizure:
If I'll get another DUI,
I'll be hanged to dry.

The wolves are fed,
The sheep are still alive;
A total paradigm, no mess,
I do continuously guess
From a weekdays' dread
To weekends' drive:
With whom to sleep
And whom to flip.

The motto of a single man
Dictates, "Get what you can,
In spite of a terrific stress:
Live, love, pay and undress!"

I have to leave this town
Before shit hits the fan;
I have to settle down
While I am still a man.

The Hymns of Lights

Remains of our crimes,
Those shattered molds
Of our astounding nights
Sing songs of our times;
We wait till darkness folds
To sing the hymns of lights,
Descending on our idle ears,
A fertile place for many years.

It is a journey,
Not a destination,
A silent tourney
Through our elation.
A day of madness
Becomes a toy,
A drop of sadness
Welcomes a new joy.

I am a fearless guard
Of intellectuals and coy,
I sold my bleeding heart
To devil's sybaritic ploy.

The stars are falling
On my shoulders,
My dreams are rolling
Like verses to my folders.

I run from those who reign,
From our heroes canonized,
Respected but not loved;
And once again
I want to be baptized
By someone velvet-gloved.

The Indian Late Summer

The rite of Indian late summer
Stops rains as a crafty plumber,
Ripens the tiny green tomatoes,
And gullible cute girls to date us.

Our anguish hits the bottom,
Our voices loud echoes rise,
And the unknown phantom
Inches us closer to paradise.

The autumn has arrived
The summer took a ride,
The muddy gush of rains
Swirls into the noisy drains.

From nowhere in my sight,
The sudden angry storms
Sway trees from side to side,
And drop their leafy uniforms.

A windy autumn blows
Great colors in its flight,
A striking rainbow flows
Across the field of light.

The naked branches reach the sky
And scratch it with their spiky nails,
The pillows of the cotton clouds fly
Like dreams under the happy sails.

Their Wreaths Fell Down

Dunes whisper to the wind,
The ebbs caress the sand,
And tease the fishing gear;
A sign "Keep off" is pinned,
Abandoned and unmanned
Sidelong the trembling pier.

The sailors went to fish,
Their wives shall wait,
Sharing a single wish,
"Return, despite the fate."

A shrimp boat reaped the storm,
And only a few seagulls swarm
Above the drowned sailors.
We love the Fisherman of souls,
And hide his faults and failures
Inside the Dead Sea Scrolls.

Poor wives may hope and wait,
But dreams will let them drown;
They will follow the old-style trait,
And climb that trembling pier,
And let their wreaths fall down.

The Foxholes of the Wars

The foxholes of the wars
Make brothers
From the Army Rangers.
Far on the foreign shores;
We fought the other brothers
Without theirs or our angels.

We know our saints,
We know our sinners,
Blood runs in our veins
Into the hearts of winners.

We are so proud of the past,
Our battles were recorded,
At times, we were awarded
Under the gloomy overcast.

They locked us in the cage
Then framed us as the arts,
And placed us on the stage
Without souls and hearts.

The shiny uniforms of heroes,
Sent our egos to the stars,
Only the smoky, dusty mirrors
Hid our wounds and scars.

Her Room is Softly Lit

Two angels sent her
To my gloomy street,
I promised to surrender
If we will ever meet.

My intuition never fails
Only the strings of rain
Spoke to the shiny rails
Devoured by the train.

Under a swirling gold,
Boogying its title role
Along the cavalcade
Of almost naked trees,
I try to cure my cold
And yet, I beg my soul,
"Please, do not fade,
I'd hate to rest in peace."

A mirror on the wall
Reflects her lovely face,
The leaves quietly fall
Into the spider's lace.

Hi, Dear, I am back;
Her room is softly lit,
My suit hangs on the rack,
Her dress falls to my feet.

Excited bride and groom
Are hopelessly insane.
A luscious smell
Of innocence in bloom,
And noisy tunes of rain
Pushed our sins to hell.

A Heavy Cloud Hides the Stars

I am never envious of fame,
I never envy those who win;
Every casino looks the same,
The tables are forever green.

Don't bring my past,
I loathe that pain,
I need some rest,
I am in a slow lane.

So many songs haven't been sung,
So many verses are unwoven,
Too late to pray, the bell has rung,
My time is up, the dice are thrown.

A heavy cloud hides the stars,
My verse is dead, I see no muse,
My soul is locked behind the bars,
Above me not a halo, but a noose.

I live the final chapter of my book,
The stars don't show me the way,
Instead, I meander, seek and look;
I hope the lights are never far away.

I know ills and I am not immune,
The healing melody is only one,
My heart is floating in that tune,
The final song of a dying swan.

The Game of Chess

We played all night,
A fight after a fight;
His Bishop took my pawn
And trapped the Queen;
He beamed like early dawn
My face turned gravely green
I was too sleepy and inept,
I badly lost and almost wept.

I love the god-sent game
Of enigmatic chess,
I failed to reach the fame,
But play, nevertheless.

Deceptive whites and blacks
Deeply involved in vicious plots
Of shy retreats and bold attacks
That cleverly connect the dots.

One day, I take it on the chin,
Next day, I dominate and win;
I don't anticipate the final round.
We play. Our hearts still pound.

The Future's Gone

My life is lying on a chopping board,
The future's gone, the past is gored,
I fell on my own sword,
My final justified award.

Gold turns into the blue,
The autumns into winters,
Only my friends pass through,
My loyal and perpetual drifters.

My soul is flying far away
Above the naked trees;
I work another gloomy day,
I am a clown on a trapeze,
But at the end, I fall
To entertain you all.

Our Platoon Marched

The guardian devils soared
Into the blameless skies
Above the killing fields of war,
Like angels in disguise.

A stairway to eternal glory
Was just an ordinary track.
It's better to be safe than sorry,
We couldn't move ahead or back.

We didn't come to leave;
We came to fight and die.
War ran us through a sieve
And hung us mercilessly to dry.
Along the valleys and the hills,
Over the fields of our futile ire,
We simply paid the bills
Of those who sent us to the fire.

My brothers walked an extra mile,
They hoped to reach safe havens;
God hadn't been here in a while,
He left us to the heartless ravens.

Our platoon marched to the sky,
Most never loved or had a drink;
We left behind our farewell sigh;
We stared ahead; we didn't blink.

Few short obituaries with our mugs,
Cold death instead of mothers' hugs,
The soulless men, who sent us here,
Have never fought, just lived in fear.

The power-holders come and go,
Only the memories forever flow.

Heaven Can Wait

I drag like a heavy cross,
Your love without passion;
The amateurs or pros,
The softness or aggression,
No one can wake you up
To sip love-nectar from a cup.

The passion of a starry night,
The grandeur of a sunny day,
May bring you back in sight,
Although you are so far away.

The pain of our farewells,
The first and happy date,
I hear the melody of rails:
Heaven can wait,
Heaven can wait,
Heaven can wait…

I look into your fiery eyes,
I touch your tender hand,
I hear your loving sighs,
I hold a wedding band.

You hide your face,
My little nightingale,
Behind the silky lace
Of a crispy bridal veil.

Your whitest dress,
Your sparkly eyes,
The beat
Of a railroad tune;

O, what a treat,
The Orient Express
Of virtues in the vice
Of our honeymoon.

My Conscious Asked

My soul's interrogation room,
A blinding, penetrating light.
My conscious asked at night,
Acting like a brand-new broom:
"The birds are graceful in flight,
The wrestlers and the boxers fight,
A flying scary witch enjoys the sight,
The spiders and mosquitoes bite,
The sun is always warm and bright.
You breathe, eat, drink and write,
Could you enjoy a gift of a simple life
Without victories in your poetic strife?"

I mumbled like a mindless bouncer,
I couldn't find a much better answer:
"From hills and valleys of my thoughts
I carve and weave my candid verses,
I rescue sailors of the sinking boats,
The oceans hear my dreadful curses
About secret charm of ancient pearls,
About dangers of honest revelations,
About innocence of optimistic girls,
About curiosities and imaginations."

Above the flowers of a virgin field,
Above the requiem for red sunset,
My dreamy castle in the sky is built,
And what I've written will be read.

I bleed for every word
Before I line them up,
I wouldn't ask my Lord
To pass by me the cup.

Nostalgia

I fought inside of ruined castles
With silence of abandoned hopes.
My tempered heart still hustles,
Bleeds like a fighter on the ropes.

Nostalgia flaunts only polished images of glee,
While melancholy strokes my miserable days,
Though, it appears as rawness versus filigree,
Both run the same dark horses in the chase.

The good old days were not that good,
Cheers of disgust ran backward to the past,
Life mended fences of my childhood,
Unhappy happy days, I buried you, at last.

My Dimly Lit Ideas

Cold winter of my soul,
Arrived as a bitter curse,
I am caged with no parole
By great but unwritten verse.

The times are sad,
The words are spoken,
The wills are written,
The hopes are dead,
The hearts are broken,
The lives are smitten.

A book of darkness over light,
A book of kindness over greed,
A book no one will ever write,
A book no one will ever read.

I am a self-deprecating villain,
I bear the pains of conscience,
My wounds are not yet healing',
Few fights, too many punches.

My hopes still wobble
Or die amid the curves,
I veer into the rubble,
I lose my weary nerves.

I am a witness of demise,
I watch the end of times:
The sun still tries to rise
Above infinity of rhymes.

I dragged my dimly lit ideas
To bathe in glory of daylight,
They said: "nobody sees us,
We are only brilliant at night."

My Double

One thing is worse than deaths:
Our lives without goals and quests,
Souls disappear with final breaths
Then reappear as uninvited guests.

The river snakes its curvy way
Between the foggy dreamy hills,
Caressing blistering red clay
With gentle bubbly spills.

Somebody peddles my canoe,
The one whom I forever knew,
He dwells and fights in me
Just short of a lethal force;
He wants to sign a treaty,
I am sure; he is the Trojan horse.

What's in the name?
Ghosts in the empty seats
Or just someone to blame
When we are caught as cheats?

I try to bathe my doctor's sin,
It complicates my sight,
I veer through thick and thin
To bait my clone into a fight.

I need to wrestle with my twin,
I bet; he is ready for the strife;
A strife that none of us can win,
But each may lose his only life.

In vain, we fought.
The wolves are fed,
The sheep are still alive,
But then, I wistfully thought:
We breathe, no one is dead,
Our hatred destined to survive.

My Dreams Long Faded

The carrier of ugly truth,
My getaway car waited
To pick my fragile youth
And dreams that faded.

Persistent vigor of my lines
Fruitfully hooks the rhymes;
I certainly express myself
Better than others on my shelf.

I am like a serpent in the grass,
I dream of castles in the clouds;
The poets made of a fragile glass
Try to avoid the merciless crowds.

My conscience being told,
"Plunge into a night of ice,
Descend from hot to cold,
Forget the ecstasy of highs."

Conscience is never far enough,
It warms me like a silky blanket,
I write about never-ending love,
The wilted flowers just flank it.

The Guillotine was Dull

We slept; it was a chilly night,
New stars got bored and fell,
Marie-Antoinette has died,
We only wished her well.

We were two city bums,
Locked in the old Bastille;
Don't send us wilted mums
If we get gravely ill.

The guillotine was dull
We both survived the blade,
Our savior, the Holy gull
Didn't allow our lives to fade.

That dire day is over:
My neck still hurts,
My limbs are lazy,
My girlfriend flirts,
She is sex-crazy.

Our shameless lies are crude,
We carry signs written in ink,
Her sign, "I'll work for food",
Mine, "Folks, buy me a drink".

We sleep under the bridge,
We have a little bit of cash,
Somebody stole our fridge,
Our eats are not too fresh.

Our income is quite stable,
We wear dark glasses,
We shake a pewter cup,
And everyone who passes,
Believes we are disabled.
Life's going on, cheer up.

No News

No news, no problems at the doors,
I am a teenager; I am still asleep.
Another day of peace without wars,
A day our mothers wouldn't weep.

An apple pie of my fantastic youth,
No filthy lies, just a lethargic truth.

Imagine lakes without swans,
It's easier to cry, than laugh,
Imagine nights without dawns,
Dark sky is just a bigger half.

I lost my mind between two lines,
I am a blind flanked by the signs.

I am a teenager, I am asleep,
A loving mother doesn't weep,
No news, her son is still alive,
A day without a deathly strife.

Upended Days

My world capsized,
It's upside-down,
I only now realized,
I used to be a king.
Today, I am a clown.

I lost my optimistic sight,
I gambled with my skin,
I took it on the chin,
And lost my final fight

The nights upended days,
More comfort for the blind,
There are no other ways,
Some lose, the others find.

A nation of shopkeepers,
Of borrowers and lenders,
Of homeless house flippers,
And morbid sex-offenders;
Forget your loud jeers,
Don't lie; you're not deaf,
Give me your idle ears,
I know the rules; I am a ref.

Please, listen; pay attention,
Ben Franklin was quite sure,
"An ounce of prevention
Is worth a pound of cure."

I begged for help my muse,
Incomprehensive Calliope,
But only sensed the blues,
She offered grief, not hope.

The Dragon

I watch my rearview mirror,
The memories don't die,
Though future is not clearer
Under the gloomy sky.

Nobody guards the gates,
The scarred king trembles,
The princess humbly waits,
The dragon boldly gambles.

The seven-headed beast
Behind the fiery glow,
Self-righteously unbind
Before his final feast;
He didn't want to know,
His bitter fate was signed.

The dragon roared fight-ready,
He waged his life at stake;
St. George rescued the lady
And got the crown in the wake
Of everlasting glory.

The end of my unneeded story.

I Pulled the Trigger

I've never seen my father,
He's never seen his son,
I've buried my old mother,
Farewell, the thrill is gone.

I have been treading water,
I hemmed and hawed,
I am ready for the slaughter,
I am a loner in the crowd.

The burning hearts
Will save the world,
The death of arts
Deletes the word.

A morning tender breeze
Across the field of lavender,
Whispers between the trees,
Your time's arrived, surrender.

My world fell in,
No place to flee,
I stay in a highway inn,
It is my unassuming glee.

I am a king without a throne,
I scrabbled in my pocket,
I pulled my gun and phone,
I shut the door and locked it.

I made my sacramental call,
I chiseled wishes in my soul,
I begged my angel to be fair;
He was distressed, not eager,
I sunk into my chair
And pulled the trigger…

I Mourn the Living

My scars are healing,
My eyes are sad,
I mourn the living,
But I forget the dead.

We face in our strife
Snake eyes of life;
We toss the dice
Across the brittle ice.

I play blackjack of life:
The aces never kill,
The sevens do,
I add sixteen to five,
I have my thrill,
I grab my win; adieu.

My single bullet gun
Is locked and loaded;
My luck is on the run,
No one yet sought it.

I begged my friend:
"I am straight as a rail,
Don't let me bend,
Don't let me fail."

I flex against the breeze
Across a sunny slope;
I am a fool on the trapeze
Above the sea of hope.

I Miss the Calm...

The fury of a dreamless slumber
Wakes up my memories at night,
A razor-lightning, a mallet-thunder
Pursue my soul. I cannot hide.

Today, I understood the game,
I can no longer sleep at all,
My hazy past demands its claim,
But I don't want to pay the toll.

I am an extra in this film,
I am not a sparkling star,
I am gray, I never gleam,
I am a badly tuned guitar.

Only in the fairytales
We are so tightly bound,
Yet pay for our affairs
The second time around.

While only the quiet rivers
Reflect the freezing skies;
It's cold; the water shivers
And we can't see our pies.

My buddies went to heaven
While I am still on cloud nine,
I am committing all the seven,
But sailing in the sea of wine.

I Never Liked Goodbyes

The sparkly earrings
Of my elusive fables
Caress your feelings
Like leaves of maples
Swirl into the freeze,
Into the calm of bliss.

I run from every dusk,
Into an inviting dawn;
I crave to peel the husk,
I will unmask the paragon:
I want to turn it on a dime,
I never trust the paradigm.

I never liked my past;
I fought and lost a war.
Today, I am falling fast,
Tomorrow, I will soar.

Some like the beatings,
Some like the cries,
I only like the greetings,
I never liked goodbyes.

Our Pathways

Even holistic views
Of dire or sinful days,
Won't have the clues
About our pathways.

Life's idiosyncratic burdens
Manipulate exasperations,
As if they're sadistic wardens
Enjoying violent intimidations.

My genially wondrous mind
Emerging on the daily scene
To hear conciliatory overture
For graveyards of the future.
I see apocalyptic horses lined
To cross the gates of paradise,
I am dazed by what I've seen,
Today, I learn to compromise.

If courage is a movie fiction
Then bravery is a conviction,
One has to overcome his fear
If anxious cowards hiding near,
Show red rags to raging bulls,
Their courage breaks the rules.

Remember, when in Rome,
Do what the Romans do,
I feel as if I am a tiny gnome
Under Saint Peter's dome.

I Never Heard the Word

I never heard the word
Which started our world.

A word is like a bird,
It's gone, it flew away
Before we ever heard,
Before we went to pray.

It flies beyond the seas
To find what we've lost,
Don't worry, please,
We'll find a new host.

A word is just a word,
What's in the name?
Goodbye, my friend,
I'll see you, mon ami.
Just shake my hand,
Today, I am also free.
End of the world?
Who is to blame?

I Never Count Chickens

I never count chickens
Before they hatch;
Until the autumn thickens,
I wouldn't use the rusty latch.

I realized that I am smart
And morphed into a normal fool;
I grabbed and threw my heart
Into a life-devouring whirlpool.

Nostalgia runs pictures of a past,
I've seen that movie many times;
Although, my scars forever last
As punishments without crimes.

I march with mop-and-bucket
Toward the tunnel's lighter end;
Time flies, I simply ducked it,
Until I am ready to ascend.

I hear a growing drumbeat
Of ancient actors' final days;
It is a time to take the heat:
I am stepping off the stage,
I am leaving lifeless plays;
A teapot whistles its head off,
My parrot's cursing in a cage.
I left my lifetime cozy trough,
And stepped into a daily blaze.

I still have a few hours to pack
My old tuxedo for the parting ball;
My best foot touched the track,
I hear the fat lady's curtain call.

I Never Knew My Saints

I never knew my saints,
I always knew my sinners,
Our memory of losers fades,
We only cherish our winners.

I notice, when I stare,
We're all equal naked,
Our souls ascending bare,
It is a fact; I didn't make it.

About forty years must pass,
Before we judge the heroes.
Sobriety descends on us,
We see ourselves dirty mirrors

Our foreverness
Is straight ahead,
Just a few moons away;
Nevertheless,
I bake some bread,
There is another day.

Don't read the signs
Of love and hate,
Delights and sorrows;
There are long lines,
They also wait;
There are tomorrows.

I Painted a Self-Portrait

I painted a self-portrait:
My vanity in a rectangle,
My features kindly sorted,
My sour fears untangled.
It was a healthy-looking truth
About my evaporating youth.

I held the horses,
My wild imagination
Has lessened
Its benchmark.
I sowed my flashy verses
But reaped a mild ovation;
Quite unexpected present
For writing "deep and dark".

Life's crawling forward only,
I can't return to yesterdays,
I am bored and I am lonely,
There's nobody to embrace.

I long for a refined someone
To face together a new dawn.
I am badly sick of metronomic
Hearts,
Of their anemic oscillography
And charts.

We have to reinvent our vowed
Paradise,
To recreate the Eden's garden
In the rough,
To climb the Knowledge tree,
To find the snake and candidly

Apologize
Then humbly beg a pardon
For punishing a tender innocence
Of love,
For kicking Adam and his Lady
From the eternity of glee.

I Own the World

The reading of guidebooks,
The idle people's notes,
Deceit of leisure travel hooks,
Deliver many rosy thoughts.

I want to walk and breathe
That fine unruffled air;
Above the fertile heath,
I need a love affair.

Here is the fruit of my desire,
I am aroused by invitation,
I saw her in a "Friends for hire",
She was so cute; I paid attention.

Besides, I reckon an advice
Once given by a stranger:
"When overseas, try to be wise,
Imagine, you just left a manger,
You learn a foreign tongue,
It shouldn't take too long,
Just sleep with your translator."
Yet use your wisdom later.

These days I have a joyous life,
I slept with my translator,
Today, she is my loving wife,
I am thankful to our creator.

Our voyages are picturesque,
We cherish our adventures,
Each is the finest arabesque
Of clouds' holding branches.

I say to critics, all of them:
"You mark my word,
I travel; thus I am,
I own the world!"

Poetic Token

Great Pegasus still meanders,
The last Apollo's naughty heir,
I run my sun-warmed fingers
Through his unruly curly hair.

I camouflage my thoughts,
I drape my moody verses,
They rock as fishing boats,
They swing as empty purses.

Life seeps somewhere away
Between my fingers every day:
Sad words have left my mouth,
Like noisy birds that left a cage;
I stomp up north or down south,
I try to curb my vicious outrage.

I live today, won't see tomorrow,
There are no years to borrow:
My life is like an unknown dance
With wildly jubilant obsession;
I've never had a second chance
To leave the first impression.

I mourn my dying love,
Again, my heart is broken.
I write as if I soar above
Inserting my poetic token:
I rearrange my words,
I braid them into strands,
I weave my edgy chords,
I give them to my friends.

Plymouth Rock

It's raining awfully hard,
A waterfall of salty tears,
I am still a skinless bard,
Walking the longest yard
Of my yet undying years.

Tongue-sharpening
In college competitions
Erased desires to prattle:
I threw away that baby
With the soapy water.
I analyze the propositions
How to win the battle
And save my rhymes
From slaughter.

I have the bluest muse,
The queen of melancholy,
The angel-savior of despair;
Why am I trying not to lose
The key to our shared glory,
To our dispassionate affair?

My boat sets sails
For a predetermined journey,
Even my incredible attorney
Won't change my mind:
Life's hanging on the thread
Holding the daily bread
For humankind.

A new era has begun,
I am no longer circling our sun,
I am in the Lord's crosshairs

Climbing the heaven's stairs.
I finally am out of the woods
And searching for that gate
Which hides from us the goods
Of souls that didn't want to wait.

I guess, I have to pick a lock
And disembark on Plymouth Rock.

Perpetual Funerals of Hopes

When is a poem finished?
When is the time to dot a line?
With fire of my heart
Extinguished,
With eyes that couldn't see
Sunshine.

Each soul has hidden corners,
Important only to the owners,
The corners that are lit at nights,
And let insights see foresights.

The corners where a black powder
Is always dry,
For those who fought and want
To fight again,
For those who have been loved
And want to cry,
For those who never served
But want to feign.

Perpetual funerals of hopes,
Rehearsals of "Amazing Grace",
Bring us to the ends of ropes,
Woven to hang, not to embrace.

Postulates

I used to turn the other cheek,
Today, I am old and better wine,
Even during the Passion Week,
I cast no pearls before a swine.

I found plenty, but I lost,
I had a lot, but couldn't save,
For friends, I am a loving host,
For foes, I dig a pleasant grave.

I hide no aces in my sleeve,
You owe me--pay the bill,
I can forget, but can't forgive,
God will…

And Bleach Them in the Sun

The spring arrived again,
A godsend timeless truth;
Destined to bear my pain,
I reap a sour fruit of youth,
I flaunt my weeping violin
I play a solo; I must win.

I am playing solo; it is a life,
Persistent as a falling knife,
I make mistakes alone,
The gig still goes on...

My tune is raw and coarse,
Impulsive as a loaded gun;
I gallop as a nervous horse,
A leaded cloud hides the sun.

I see the firebirds of hope,
I touch the fountains of fun,
I tie my sorrows with a rope
And bleach them in the sun.

I know, love will find me,
Wild as flowers in the grass,
The greatest feast of glee
With happiness in every glass.

My solo is a lifelong strive,
I am a bee that lost his hive;
I miss the tune; I am alone,
The play must go on...

But at the End

We split some hairs,
And drown in sophism,
Under the dusty layers
Of a pessimistic nihilism.

I hold the enigmatic gem
With secrets of the word.
I am at the mighty helm,
I search the underworld:
Solemnity of laughter,
Sobriety of quiet cries,
The mornings after,
The frailty of lives.

Two lovers at the window,
Two shadows on the floor,
They aimed quite high
Into the brightest glow;
In vain, they tried to fly,
But drowned in the flow.

These loves don't cry,
They break our hearts,
Their wings don't fly,
They only send regards.

I bravely run and zig,
I humbly walk and zag
Over the shattered lives,
Under a hand-made wig
With a hand-written tag,
Glued to the other lies.

I met my oldest friend,
Those days were gray;

We swam in wine,
But at the end
Of every drunken day
We'd never cross the line.
Long live
The rhythms of our lives,
Our self-imposed routines,
Our teardrops in the wines,
The joy of our forgiven sin.

I Solved the Riddle

I walked into a foyer
With a sign "court in session",
The laws slid even lower
Than our faked compassion.

I am Mary Magdalene
From the Magdala town;
I could become a queen
And wear a bridal gown,
But walked my extra mile,
I dated Jesus for a while.

Imagine doubts of his father,
Who never had another kid,
He knew, but didn't bother,
His son will love and bleed.

The winds of change
Don't change a lot
Within a fiery range
Of our Big bang plot.

Under the guise of truth
I found lies,
Under the veil of good,
I found evil.
I heard the loud laughs
Above the cries,
Under a turning globe
I saw a broken swivel.

I had to wash my eyes
To thread the needle,
I paid a hefty price,
But solved that riddle.

We try to solve our puzzles,
But never mind the troubles.

I Shuffled Out

My Sunday Mass
Gave its respond
In future tense.
I hope the grass
Is green beyond
A mended fence.

I can no longer bear
The childish nihilism
Of a constant squawk;
Besides a lion's share
Of snobbish mannerism
And rivers of small talk.

A bunch of graph maniacs
Wrote thousands of books;
They flourished while I bled.
I am edgy with the quacks,
With greedy literary crooks,
Who steal my daily bread.

The art of giving is a bunch of lies
That makes me realize the truths,
Beyond my muted sighs and cries,
Beyond the graves of wasted youths.

I thought, the end is near,
And shuffled out of old age,
Back into my bookish past;
Today, I say what everyone
Deserves to hear;
I found on the closing page
God's primal word, at last.

I Stir the Sediments

I stir the sediments
In bottles of my days,
The rising sticky fear
Erases sentiments…
Yet wrinkles on my face
Appear divinely clear.

The colorless moonlight
Runs like a horror movie,
The shades dispose of light,
Obscurity is rather gloomy.

My gruesome yoke of fate,
You're a brute gendarme,
I loathe your dreadful trait,
I'll fight you tooth and nail,
Don't waste your charm,
Where is the Holy Grail?

I talked myself into a fight,
And swung at every pitch,
I lived the longest night,
But soothed my itch.

The path to bliss is paved,
The baby steps are taken,
A boisterous crowd raved,
Eternity is in the making.

I kissed goodbye the day,
I waved farewell at night,
My paradise is on the way,
Long live the luring light.

I Led Her to Sunset

I acted as a puppeteer
Over a cute marionette;
I led her to a red sunset,
But found just a nook,
She gave me all. I took.

It was our first sunset,
It was our first real night,
She thought it was a debt,
I thought it's my birthright.

She was a bird in hand…
I whispered common lies,
She soared over the land,
Skies mirrored in her eyes.

Symphonic coexistence
Of our independent plays,
Of our days and nights;
Peace walks the distance,
While Nike humbly prays
Before our vicious fights.

She wore a shawl of irony,
I wore a jacket of despair;
That war of rage and glee,
We could no longer bear.

Goodbye, Be Well

The foreign flags
Flap in the breeze,
The tourists drag their bags
And fight the evening freeze.

I walk along the river's flow,
I stroll across the ancient park,
I'm from Nashville to say hello,
But Moscow sleeps; it's dark.

A country scraps; it's only fair,
The city didn't lose its flair;
The old regime is banished,
The pedestals without heroes,
Some villains fell and vanished
Into the fog of smoky mirrors.

The anxious city of my birth,
The honey-river of the past,
The sweetest place on earth,
Nostalgic youth arrived, at last.

Old Russia hides behind the walls,
New USA with lures of freedom;
I shared my life between two souls-
I lost my folly, gained my wisdom.

I waved my hand,
Goodbye, be well-
I crossed the land to say farewell
To heavy burdens of the past.
I wave my hand, goodbye, be well,
I am forever free, at last.

My Eyes Were Peeled

True words remain unwritten,
The world remains lie-smitten.

My eyes were peeled
For butts and chests,
For legs well healed
And all the rest…

The night walks through the street,
My verses choke beneath its feet;
Only the young are still naïve,
They think I am a poet, not a thief.

The words are silent like the mimes;
I stroll and carefully pick them up,
They've been in use so many times;
I sheepishly collect them in my cup.

My arms turn out to be wings:
I write for you, my quiet world
The words no one yet heard,
Against the blow of headwinds.

I Shook a Fruitless Tree

I was born to die
And I am dead,
But later even resurrected;
It's written in the Book
I've read,
My caring Mom selected.

I didn't seek the fame,
I shot the devil's clone
And not a day too soon.
They carved my name
On the precious stone,
Fallen from the moon.

I shook a fruitless tree;
I am poor; I have a witness;
Life never shared with me
Its god-sent sweetness.

I suffered all my life
As an abandoned dog;
I didn't learn to drive,
I didn't learn to smoke,
I didn't have a hidden plan;
They locked me in the can.

And lastly, I am free;
They checked the DNA's,
But didn't like my pedigree,
I only hear their constant nays.
It is a time to have some rest.
The gods are usually almighty,
But not at the day of my arrest.

They sent me their apologies,
Annoying as the dirty glasses.
My shrink twisted a mythology,
My lawyer stuck it to their asses.
Only my thankless dog still yelps;
I swig my lavish life. Money helps

I Run My Final Lap

I am waiting for the train,
Nothing arrives, but rain.

Free cheese waits
Only in the trap,
I loathe my dates,
I run my final lap.

I play the game of chess,
Whites plan a vigorous
Attack,
Blacks build a strong
Defense,
The queen lifts up her
Dress,
The clumsy king crawls
Back,
Pawns have no common
Sense.

Sweet dreams
Become nightmares
When sunlight gleams,
When moonlight flares.

The second mouse
Gets the cheese,
The early bird
Gets fatter worms.
I bet against the house,
I dress the naked trees,
I'm a disillusioned nerd,
No essence, only forms.

The frog expects the kiss,
The cat is out of the bag,
The dog enjoys the play,
The sun lights the abyss
The dancer breaks a leg,
The spring is on the way.

I See no Corners...

Two candles died,
Sunset took over,
Only the clouds glide
Above the fields of clover.
Back then, I lived alone,
My nightmares owned me:
I was a king who lost his
Throne,
I was a whale who drowned
In his sea.

I gather every hug and kiss
Of strangers' gloomy lives;
I heal and cheer them;
I take them to my bliss
To those amazing hives
Next to a Holy Bethlehem.

Again, a heavy burden fell
On my scarred shoulders;
I push from bliss to hell
Sisyphean boulders.

I bet, my foes remember me,
While many have forgotten;
They love the years of glee,
But mourn over the rotten.

The piercing strings of rain
Run by my wrinkles-grooves,
Rinsing illusions of those days.
I am sprinting from this maze,
Cursing my tattered hooves.

I walk and run, I fly and ride
Among the chatty mourners;
Fat singing lady is quite near,
I need a cozy place to hide,
But couldn't see dark corners
In our god sent atmosphere.

I'll Sing the Songs I Know

The torment of my fight sets me on fire-
I write as if I work in circus on the wire.
My line is crude that once was tender,
I still enjoy my words; I won't surrender.

No one is right, no one is wrong,
Though love gets more uncertain;
Love is a new, and unknown song,
I'll write it till the final curtain.

An apple thrived
On conversations
Before Adam and Eve arrived.
They ate the fruit;
God lost his patience,
And our first duo got the boot.

I need to meet someone
Before my muse is gone,
I long for everlasting love,
I want to be a loving dove

I'll sing the songs I know,
Only this night is dormant.
The day will thaw the glow
Of my life's frozen torrent.

I Peeled Dense Shadows

My world is like a fable,
I outlined it on the map,
Then put it on the table
And used it as a wrap.

I peeled dense shadows
Off the fruitless grounds,
And liberated wilted fruits
From the garden bounds.

Through weary blankets
Youthful blades of grass
Pierce nightly darkness,
Refute the futile dogmas,
Tighten the multicolored
Ribbons beautifying gifts;
The gifts of gentle hopes,
The gifts of fearless love,
The gifts of fiery passion
Carrying delicious meals
Of curiosity and intellect,
Integrity and imagination.

Nobody ever understands
Tongue-twisting speakers;
The demagogic squeakers
Pull rabbits from their hats
While our working classes
Enjoy their empty glasses.

Our pedantic world at work
Blows apart a mighty night;
A trembling beam of dawn
Summons a childless stork,

Requests a courteous swan
To sing about blinding light.

A dying swan, a final breath,
It is our dawn, it is his death.

I played in Bands

I played in bands,
I walked on Mars,
I stretched my life,
I stirred quite fast,
I raked loose ends,
I dumped my wife,
I touched the stars,
I burned my hands,
I smashed my cast,
I went through bars,
I lied to you in vain,
I lost my final strife,
I knew I was insane,
I left my ended past,
I wrapped my scars,
The wounds remain.

I Pour Dead-Ends

I pour dead-ends of our lives
In every offered to me glass;
I listen to new cries and sighs;
Red velvet of a luscious wine
Reflects much greener grass
Belonging to a friend of mine.
I think I am unjustly left alone,
I hold a bag of bitter sorrows,
I think I have to make a clone
Who takes, but never borrows;
So hard to pace the top alone,
So hard to walk on feet of clay,
So hard to cast a primal stone,
My foes still fly above the fray.

I jumped through many hoops,
I crossed too many futile lines,
I simply mumbled "oops"
While gliding pass stop signs.

I'd picked a low hanging fruit,
Knowing it's not the very best,
It's a free lunch; it's just a loot,
For homeless and well dressed.

My gluttony is a lifelong joy,
Unbearable as a chronic pain,
I am a part of a satanic ploy,
My scientific efforts are in vain;
Artistic grounds are not broken,
I am a loser: God has spoken.

I touch the sky,
The clouds cry,
I'd rather bend
And touch the land.

I Paid a Gorgeous Girl to Strip

I left the filthy motel rooms
And joined exciting masses
Of the intelligent discourse
Inhaling marihuana fumes,
Sipping from tinkling glasses
And chewing Hors d'oeuvres.

The day of reckoning is here,
Fiction and history will merge,
The truths rest on a higher tier,
The lies will undergo a purge.

Better than fire sale prices
Allows me a luscious dinner.
Anticipation of a midlife crisis
Creates a loser from a winner.

In quest for far-off treasures
Even Columbus sunk a ship.
In quest for carnal pleasures
I paid a gorgeous girl to strip.

It's absolutely different with me:
I pay for sex and say goodbye,
Then live in this perpetual glee
Escorted by the finest lullaby,
"When making love was just
For fun,
Those days have gone…"

Is it a star descending
From the sky?
It is a teardrop running
From my eye.

Back Home from War

I am drinking poisons
Of vanity and greed,
Then roll and moisten
A joint of great weed.

I am still dreaming of
Rose-colored love,
Blue birds of hope,
Black paws of death
Pulling a lumpy rope
Over my final breath.

I dive headlong into
A seductive lightness
Of downtown nights;
Truths bring sunrises,
Possessing blinding
Brightness of a quest
By egotistical insiders
For the emerging sun.

Today, I am knocking
On the door,
Who's there? It's I,
Back home from war
Under the bloody sky.
My fate is sealed,
Watch, I am wheeled,
Wrapped in the flag,
Just check the toe tag.

Years came and went,
The facts erased,
The history rewritten,

The bridges burned,
The constitution bent,
New generation raised,
New regulations written,
But nothing ever learned.

I Trust in Earthly Paradise

We were two perfect strangers,
Two young, but wingless angels;
You shyly pulled your lacy dress,
"Come close, don't double guess."

I wanted to inhale the dreamy scent
Of your unblemished virgin breast;
I crossed the Rubicon of my intent,
And slid far down to the rest…

I sense, I am a go-getter,
I point as a hunting setter,
I trust in earthly paradise,
While I am fond of daily lies.

I whipped my dusty crystal ball,
I made an epic trusty daring call.
Somewhere, someone
Prays on his quiet glee,
Somewhere, someone
Promises more to me.

He shared his glee,
I promised him my heart,
I am chained, he is free;
He trumped my card.
From time to time I love or hate,
I coexist with my illusionary fate.

I Wade Across the River

I wade across the river,
Stomp to the other side;
The day is cold, I shiver,
But I'll see my love tonight.

There is another bridge,
The one I want to burn.
Don't ever ask me which;
Please wait, I shall return.

A little table in the garden,
We're talking in the shade;
The sun is slowly sliding,
Our illusions quickly fade.

Out of seven wonders of the world,
You are the first, just mark my word.
You don't believe in amiable stories,
Wake up, loves die amid our worries.

The night is young and long,
Give me the one and only chance.
I'll never do you wrong
Before or after your bridal dance.

Serenity

The whiny trains
Of an old railway
Run noisy rains
Into my misty day.

I hardly close my eyes,
I never miss the boons
Of quiet gloomy skies
And enigmatic moons.

I love these lonely nights
Without wrongs or rights,
Without friends and foes,
Without poetry and prose.

Here is my true identity,
I am a man of solitude:
I choose a short serenity
Against an endless feud.

Prologue

My resume had lines
About special skills,
I humbly wrote alcoholism.
I guzzle scotch and wines,
Then soberly accept my thrills
I see them through a rosy prism.

First item every morning,
Last thing before I fall asleep,
I see a dusty copy of a sculpture.
A mother in her mourning,
Who still continues to weep
Over her son's divine departure.

I cannot drink a filtered water,
I drink cheap beers and wines
Before warmonger's saber-rattling,
Before the other slaughter,
Before the bombs and mines,
Before insane absurdity of battling.

Life-saving warning sighs
Of my arriving heart attack,
Neglected by my heavy boozing,
Sun-craving morning signs
Of the pontificating Zodiac,
Are lining doctors of my choosing.

This planet is too crowded
For all of us,
Some will depart to heaven,
But most must crawl to hell,
Let's flip a quarter,

I call the tails
And never wonder
Whether my fortune
Thrives or fails…

She Was a Perfect Trooper

Among the nightly wizards,
She was a gutsy alligator,
Among the lounge lizards
She was the fastest waiter,
Even in a drunken stupor
She was a perfect trooper.

She cursed between her laughs,
I liked it very much, it was iconic;
Her life-size naked photographs
Where powerfully quadraphonic;
She barked her filthy paragraphs,
They were entertaining and ironic.

I tossed the dice
And won the prize,
I held her in my arms,
Devouring her charms.

I am a hunter; I eat my kill,
I am a man; I need a thrill,
Most women want but wait,
Most men just take the bait.

Spring quickly flew away,
I dared to call her in July,
I brought her a bouquet,
I wore my only suit-and-tie
And wanted her to say,
"Your flowers will never die."

Old-fashioned Hats

Our bodies take cold showers,
Our souls prefer hot baths,
They purify the sins of wraths;
Meanwhile almighty powers
Disseminating fruitless bits
Of our watered-down wits.

Our wisdom is already dead,
Our madness learned to walk,
Eagerly devours our daily bread,
While we are doing our small talk.

A rearview of our experience
Flaunts our visions of the past,
We hide behind glossy exteriors
Of our conscience on probation,
While our minds are in the cast,
As victims of evolution of creation,
They wear old-fashioned hats
Of their intellectual castration.

Prelude

I am just a musical quicksand:
A scherzo of Johannes Brahms
Played by the marching band
Under a brassy coat of arms.

I watch those women,
Who labor on the farms
Of carnal pleasures,
With those greed-driven
Interwoven charms
Of our priceless treasures.

I sin, confess and dream,
I even dust my weary soul;
The vultures soar and wait,
The angry seagulls scream.
The heaven's teardrops roll
Into my thirsting fate.

The flare of lightning bolts
Morphs nightmares into light,
While thousands of volts
Create a gap that daily widens
Within the everlasting fight
Of evil versus hallowed guidance.

Please, Stop the Earth

Please, stop the Earth,
It is a scorching stove,
I cannot take it anymore,
After you gave me birth;
I took a few years off
Until you shut the door
Into the blinding lights,
Into the vicious storms,
Into the bloody fights,
Into the starry swarms.

Give me a break,
A shot in the arm,
For goodness sake,
I miss Parisian charm.

The old Seine river…
Its lazy ripples rock
The willows' limbs
Into the red sunrise.
In elegant demeanor,
I walk a squeaky dock,
A haven for my whims,
My virtues and my vice.

Merci,
Rue Rivoli,
Grand rivière Seiné,
C'est bon très bien.

Parisien surprise ?
C'est mon paridis.

Parisian Delightful Dead Ends

Parisian delightful dead ends:
I asked her, ''Do you want me?''
She said, ''Let's just be friends'',
In French a brushoff is soyons aimis.

I was a raging bull with pointed horns,
But never touched that trembling rose;
Much later someone pulled her thorns,
He took the poetry and left the prose.

I live as a charge d'affaires
Of that exhilarating fairytale
Studded with the fleur de lis;
I hide, but can no longer bear
My run from yet another bail,
Somebody has to pay the bill.

I am like a puffing locomotive
Chugging along the railing lines,
I move with no apparent motive,
I am confused and agonized…
My wheels drum out olden dreams,
My newer verses hardly look divine,
They rush like the naughty streams,
They are afraid of being canonized.

I saw the burning bush, I heard that voice,
While watching ladies of the Moulin Rouge,
My dicey choice; I'd rather date the babies.

It takes all hands-on deck,
To turn my life around,
I am ok, I am not grave bound,

Although, I am a total wreck.
The morning sun has risen,
But early leaded overcast
Buried the future from my past.

Our Magic Flight

We knew the truth, our wishes perish,
We pardon errors and sweet illusions
Of our guilty youth; we didn't cherish
The broken arrows of grim confusions.

Our first kiss, never too soon,
The real bliss under the moon
No one regrets, no one forgets.

Two loves, a stolen night,
We were alone, two doves,
Two angel's wings. We are too naïve
For our magic flight through fiery rings.
No aces in the sleeve,
I simply held her tight.

It's awfully cold. It's all she wrote.
The ice already seized her quote
Into the sacred concealed mold.

After the cross of love
A few get resurrected,
The fate's crosshairs
Was the expected end
For those who truly lived
Or only shrewdly acted.

Straight as Rain

The moon still gleams,
I am relaxed and doze,
I lead my hazy dreams
From poetry to prose.

My tired good old train
Complains and sighs;
But I am straight as rain,
I crave much kinder skies.

I am entrenched on Earth,
The cozy cradle of my birth
With flowers and berries,
With mountains and fields,
With rivers and the ferries,
Amid the stops and yields.

I need someone to kiss;
I am requested into bliss.

She Was a Working Girl

I guess it was the time for me to fail,
I looked for peace in a quiet haven,
I combed through every little street,
Unfortunately, in vain, to no avail,
I looked for angels, I met a raven,
I wonder who arranged this treat.

I meandered down here; she flew,
We looked into each other's eyes,
No feathers roughed, no injured pride,
We knew, we both were in disguise,
We were interrelated; here is a clue:
Her skin was black. I was black inside.

I wrote like every poet
My sermon on the mount
As the whole-hearted songs.
It was a perfect moment
To keep a strong account
Of what was rights or wrongs.

I wrote it for this charming raven,
This pretty, but ill-mannered girl,
This Orleans' scorched maiden,
Mysterious in her majestic role,
I trembled, I was eager to unfurl
The banner of her heart and soul.

She was a working girl,
She gave me what I asked;
She was a precious pearl
Magnificent, but masked.

As in the story of Magdalene,
Nobody dared to cast a stone,
She was so innocently clean.
The gods and saints still moan.

Solitaire

Highways of life were empty,
There was no one to race,
I pulled a crumbled twenty
With Andrew Jackson's face
And carefully rolled a straw…

I knew the boundaries of law,
This time, I didn't cross the line.
I had no doubts and regrets,
I used to be the fastest draw,
My life was hanging on a twine,
I paid my dues in full, no debts.

A life is still a highway to nowhere,
I am chugging forward like a train;
At times, I play a game of Solitaire
Then try to cure my chronic pain.

I stroll along the mighty Maples
Shedding their golden leaves,
I wonder, can they grow apples
To sweeten my inevitable griefs.

My efforts crossed the spectrum
Between the rhymes and prose,
Although, my editor rejects them,
They never go away, just pause.

I confiscated my uneven writing
From brutally malignant critics,
I am sick and tired of their biting.
I hate those brainless paralytics.

I burned my verses and my fables,
My horses left the burning stables.

Rain Dribbles in the Dark

I took someone's advice,
Take virtue, not the vice,
I followed; it was wrong,
Nobody sang that song.

The birds desert the sky,
Rain dribbles in the dark,
The sweaty windows cry,
They miss a rainbow arc.

The thunders roar,
The clouds ramble,
I pace the shaky floor,
The shadows tremble.

I am usually alone
And learn much more
Than meets the eye:
Life is a combat zone,
I let my worries soar
Into the friendless sky.

I can no longer bear
This gruesome night;
I am a bard of the affair
Amid the dark and light.

My Blue-Eyed Pond

My blue-eyed pond, you are my muse,
My magic wand, my devastating blues.

Compassion rules the world,
Inspired by our loving hearts,
By problems of the real word,
By the sheer obscurity of arts.

Until my thoughts deserted me forever,
Until the clockwork of my weary heart
Stopped making its mystifying noises,
I tore apart the hair thin lifelong thread
That braiding me with fates and faiths,
Dreams, hopes and laughs of people;
My fingertips felt their lackluster pulse,
My ears heard words of the beginning,
I viewed my angels in the thick of night,
I ran and fell before I climbed the wall,
I saw the burning bridge of yesterdays.
And saw a quiet death of my own past.

I'll cross the street;
I'll walk the sunny side;
I'll tolerate the heat;
I'll learn to run and hide.
It never crossed my mind
I need a quiet cozy shade;
I'll swallow vanity and pride;
I'll leave the stage and fade.
I'll have no one to blame;
I'll withdraw from the game;
I'll erase my tarnished name
From the quagmire of fame.

I'll leave my soul; I'll sell my flesh,
I'll fall and crawl; I'll take the cash.
I'll never reach the clouds;
I'll never touch the stars;
I'll be lonely in the crowds;
I'll dwell behind the bars.
I'll part the gloom from the fanfare;
I'll reach the floor of the abyss,
I'll seek the darkness of despair,
Then, only then, I'll ascend to bliss.

No Longer Hell

Reality and arts at war,
I loathe the bloody sky
Over my long farewell.
I slam our heavy door,
Emotions drain me dry,
I am leaving daily hell.

I sowed a red sunset,
And reaped a fiery sky,
I saw death's silhouette,
I watched but didn't cry.

The heartfelt altruism
Created silly orders:
The rubble of cubism
Erected foggy borders,
The sins of modernism
Destroyed the hurdles.

The pit of the abyss,
The dome of bliss
Reviled a water well,
Life was no longer hell.

Art was a road to nowhere,
I didn't argue, I didn't dare.

No Crack of Light

I haven't seen our bliss
Or their abyss,
I haven't seen daylight
Between the two.
At first, I heard the word,
I didn't see a crack of light
Before the Lord
Got through.

My stubbornness and pride
Won't push my dreams aside:
My flesh wants Pere Lachaise,
My soul is fated to that craze.

The fish rot from the head down,
A wet god Neptune has no shoes
To lose,
But he may drop his royal crown
If he will get a chance to choose.

I ditched my comfortable life
And funneled my attention
To precious inorganic objects,
To relics of my farewell strife,
To witnesses of my dissension
With all those sybaritic intellects.

While Peter-Paul keep gates ajar,
I watch the morning guiding star,
I strike a final parting on my guitar,
And wave to all of you au revoir.

Life isn't black and white,
There's no daylight
Between their bliss
And our abyss.

No Chastity in Me

The lightning divided
My thoughts in half,
Entirely equal parts,
The others sided
With reality,
I sided with the arts.

I looked for the elusive
gene,
I ripped apart my DNA,
I split morality from its
hygiene
and found my own way.

I saw the Prince of Peace
And Light,
And changed forever since:
It was Palm Sunday night
Red carpets faded,
Palms wilted,
The history was raided
The truth was tilted.

It was the light of dawn
That didn't want
To morph into a sunny day.
That day, I acted as a fawn,
A futile beast on feet of clay
Without anything to flaunt.
I rang the bell until it melted
Under the brutal loving sun,
I fell, my soul was dented;
Most enigmatic hit-and-run.

Don't look for chastity in me,
I am not Mary who gave birth
Being completely pure.
When gods created
Us on Earth,
They didn't make
Our integrity carefree,
Yet didn't leave the cure.

No Solace in My Strife

War is a pain for each,
Peace is a glee for all,
I know which is which,
Our world is truly small.

Why is it so hard to sleep
In a soft bed of life?
Why is it so hard to keep
Integrity in our daily drive?

Each wrinkle-riverbed
Of mother's tears,
Each mourns the dead,
Each buries fears,
So we can climb the walls
To reach our higher goals.

No solace in my strife,
No help from the above,
No friends to lose;
I prize my grievous life
But when I'll have enough,
I'll just drown in my booze.

Push came to shove,
I learned to hate,
I didn't learn to love
Until I saw the holy gate.

Paul, Use Your Head

It is a self-defeating fight,
Just a lackluster thrill
Over the black and white
Of my yet unsigned will.

My grandma said,
"Paul, use your head,
Don't sign, don't be a shark,
At night, it is too dark,
Wait for the lights,
You will enjoy the sights:
They dream of winning big,
You dream of losing small,
It is endurance
Of this intrigue,
It is insurance
Covering us all."

They tried, but couldn't find,
I left no fingerprints behind,
The witness was a mime,
He saw, but never testified,
It was a perfect crime,
A fallen angel was my guide.

My grandma said,
"Paul, use your head."

She is My Unwritten Page

Glee dwells in yesterdays,
Occasionally, in tomorrows
Abandoning today.
The past appears as daily
Holidays,
The future as a joy without
Sorrows,
The present as an eternal
Maze.

I loved
Her hungry, luscious lips,
I loved
Her cheery, joyous mood,
Then why
I've met the four horsemen
Of the apocalypse,
Before
My guarding spirit knocked
On wood.

Insomnia's alarming light
Cast demons on my soul.
Another sleepless night,
Another starry waterfall.

Even a lethargic sleep
May end someday,
I learned to laugh,
I learned to weep,
I learned to sin,
But couldn't learn to pray.

My loneliness is horrid,
I miss her on the stage,
She isn't sad or worried,
She simply left my cage.

She left that quiet nook
Without tears of outrage,
I am her unopened book,
She is my unwritten page.

Short Days, Long Nights

A clown reads my rights,
The courtroom dreary farce,
Stiff words of sound bites,
Long days, short nights.

This is my life, it is my solo,
I flew too high but fell too low.
I did my utmost, I tried my best,
I am not a host; I am just a guest.

I am caged with cattle,
I won some fights,
But lost the final battle;
Short days, long nights.

In dreams I breathe,
Only in dreams I run
And win the wreath,
Burned with the sun.

The end is near; I am here on loan,
I pawned my fear; I am here alone.

The death row silent blues:
No arguments, no fights,
There's nothing else to lose,
Short days, short nights.

Shy People Hide or Crawl

Shy people hide or crawl
Away from danger,
Try to avoid eternal brawl
Of us versus a fallen angel.
It is dialectics of resistance:
We see the tears or grins,
Small steps, long distance,
It's still a draw; no one wins.

I was like a church's mouse
Who played a twenty-one
Against the mighty house,
And lost it all before a dawn.

I fire at people verbal darts
Soaring away from players,
Who want me for a song
Until they change their hearts:
I learn from my good prayers,
I shall return to play. So long.

I'll return as a crude stranger
And pull a ten to ace,
I'll become a calm avenger
With pressure over grace.

I felt the brunt
Of truths and lies,
It took an acrobatic stunt
From the inertia of ice,
From harbor of a sleeping pill
Into a shining city upon the hill.

I won't ascent on every mount,
My pride and vanity no more,
I'll battle only what may count
And win my private war.

Slowdown, Iron Horse

Slowdown, iron horse,
Please, take it easy,
Look how many whores
Lined up and freezing.

Here is my basic plan,
I do this now and then:

I'll pick a nice and cute,
I'll pick the very best;
She'll play my flute
And disregard the rest.

I'll tell her: please,
Turn off the key,
Sit still and wait,
Watch the police,
Immediately flee
Before it is too late.

I'll lock the door,
Adjust the seat,
If nothing more,
I'll like the treat.

She'll slowly bend,
I've seen that show,
She'll jerk by hand
Then kiss and blow.

She was quite cute,
She played my flute.

Short Summer Rain

Short summer rain,
Long lazy stream,
The strands of pain
Poured to the rim.

A worthless flight,
The weary shrouds
Hover my dreams,
Another pretty sight
Between the clouds,
Along the beams.

I am cold,
The weary sun
Can't warm
Me anymore.
No time to fold,
No time to run
Before the storm,
Before another war.

My wisdom wasn't cheap,
I dearly paid for every bit
Of this gigantic leap;
The stairway to heaven
Wasn't lit.

I burned a sky-high pile
Of wishes and desires,
Ignited by my smile
And vanities' bonfires.

She Has Become My Wife

I wouldn't change skylines,
I couldn't change the trends,
I paid my never-ending fines
And tried to meet the ends.

It was a splendid jolly night,
White tie and tails attire,
And suddenly, I saw the light,
My heart was set on fire.

She has become my wife,
I didn't earn that great award,
She fell into my boring life
From heaven like a firebird.

She is my loving wife no more,
She walked and shut the door.

Aloneness is not a quick death,
Aloneness is a leisurely decay;
Before bliss gets my breath,
Before I hug my parting day,
I hope to kiss her one more time
Before I am in sacred paradigm.

No one has ever seen
My weary soul's teardrops,
When lives are evergreen,
We only yield, nobody stops.

She Firmly Marches Over

She firmly marches over,
Her heels unkindly poke
The virgin field of clover
Under the morning's cloak.

There is no time to weep,
There is no place to leap,
There is no time to think,
There is no place to drink,
There is no time to plea,
There is no place to flee,
There is no time to talk.
There is no place to walk.

I am tired of your spurs,
I am so tired of my pain,
I am a poet, not a horse,
My verse won't die in vain.

Running of the Bulls

I never lay across the rails,
I never strode on rusty nails,
I never robbed the graves,
I never made huge waves.

One day, I was invited
To Pamplona, Spain,
I have decided
To misuse my brain:
I'll be running with the bulls,
As one of those damn fools.
My apathetic life has ended,
My Spanish jet has landed.

The sun will also rise
Above the narrow streets
Of stampedes and retreats.
Dear armchair matadors,
Take words of my advice,
Don't leave your corridors,
Watch from the balconies,
Climb on the roof, it's free,
Don't try to run, just flee,
Leave rampage to the bulls,
To runners from themselves,
To those red-tied dumbbells.

I bravely ran before the bulls,
Amid daredevils and the fools;
It was a thrill, no one to blame,
Next year, I'll repeat the same.

Scottish Whisky

I drink with faceless crowds,
I think I am a mockingbird,
I entertain the lonely clouds,
They hear my slurred absurd.

I am a rose without petals,
I am a bird without wings,
I am a bike without pedals,
I am a phone without rings.

I sip my Scottish whisky,
Another much-too-risky,
I cannot stop, I only hold.
I burn my troubled soul,
Barflies don't ever fold,
We fall into black hole.

I am up before the dawn,
Half sober, widely yawn,
The wrinkles of a dread
Slide down my forehead.

A glass of Bloody Mary
A bitter coffee in a bowl:
Each is a good old fairy,
I wish them best of all.

I am beyond the cure,
I am a boat without a sail,
I am a bride no longer pure,
I am whisky in the Holy Grail.

I tease my troubled soul,
I build my paradise on Earth,
I sip my Scottish whisky till I fall
It is my mother's milk since birth.

The Last Train Station

The last train station,
I bought a one-way ticket,
The last translation,
Into the plain from wicked.

I won't be back,
I left this shore,
I pass my own track,
Not a revolving door.

I am a sinner, a godsend:
Beyond the thrown dice,
Beyond the given word,
Beyond the bidding hand
I see the Promised Land
I see the bridges burned,
I see eternity I earned,
I see the gate of paradise,
I see the sinless world,
I see my future at the end.

A Lonely Happy Hour

I tossed away my key
To a safe haven,
I am in the daring fight
Against a raven,
Rebellion is never free,
The nightmares
Visit me at night.

A lonely happy hour,
I am a buzzer beater;
I cannot play softball,
No skills and power,
But as a baby sitter
I robbed Saint Peter
And paid Saint Paul.

The windows glow
Through the frost,
The sparkly snow
Being a cozy host
Embraced my day,
The rite of spring
Is on the way:
The perky grass,
The singing birds
A luscious wine
In a crystal glass
And empty words.

I am happy in my nest,
I strive and do my best,
I want to live tomorrow;
I gamble and don't fold,
If I am broke, I borrow.
I bluff and boldly hold.

The Madness of a Solstice

The madness of a solstice,
The murky sun is farthest
Or nearest to our equator,
I am praying on my knees,
Inviting malice to my quest,
Expecting, "See you later."

Life is a bow-legged hooker,
I dwell between her legs,
I try to be a forward-looker;
I buy my joy; she only begs.

I laugh to imitate the Hell,
I cry to imitate a Holly bliss,
Life didn't treat me well,
I earned my rest in peace.

I see my fortune's tired eyes,
Mirroring pain of futile hopes;
The fallen angel in disguise
Wants me to walk tightropes.

He pulls and splits my hair,
Whipsaws my mind in half;
I am convinced he will dare
To dig my grave and laugh.

Axiomatic good is still alive,
It is complete and necessary,
And worthy of a bloody strive
For I am believing in a fairy.

Fire-breathing dragons rattle;
My soul and body set ablaze;
It is a great Apocalyptic battle,
And seems like the end of days.

The Mermaids' Village

The Mermaids' village
By daring Paul Delvaux,
Manifestation of a dream.
Lack of a single cleavage
Collects my feelings' flow,
The eyes reflect my gleam.

Their hearts were looted
Through trials-and-errors,
I flew as a hopeless cupid
Tossing my aimless arrows.

Art lovers vigorously cast
The shades of silhouettes
On tatty tapestries of time;
The future's murky past
Embezzled our futile bets
On punishment and crime.

I walk, I run, and crawl,
I am navigating doubts,
Avoiding my beliefs.
I try to break the wall
Between what-now's
And what-ifs.

Don't wake me up,
Allow me to burn,
I am in paradise;
God passed that cup,
I wasted all I earned.
My angel threw the dice.

The Mirror of a Lake

You are my wedding band,
You hold my craving hand,
You are my treasure island,
My sweet oasis in the sand.

The band kept playing,
The tango filled the room,
Your eyes were saying,
"I love you, be my groom."

All our lies were sieved
By mirrors of eternal love,
Our future was relieved
By the alluring sky above.

Above the mirror of a lake
The storms are on the make,
The greatest mystery of art
'Till death sets us apart.

The old lies won't be grieved,
The new ones will be weaved.

Death is a Pricey Whore

Life is cheap; it is a war,
Death is a pricey whore.

These days, I am free,
But yet against the wall,
I am bouncing the ball,
I count one, two, three.
My faith began to dwindle
At the dusk of life;
I am in doubt,
I am rotating on a spindle
As if I am a chunk of clay
Before the red-hot drought.

In vain, I search for answers
Nights and days,
Life doesn't offer a free lunch,
One always pays;
It helps to know how much.

It was the kiss of death,
I kissed life with a slug
Between her lazy eyes;
I heard her final breath.
She wanted just to mug,
But finished on the ice.

It took a while,
I stride and smile,
I wear a stupid hat,
I wear a birthday suit,
The end of my pursuit,
I am happy; I am fat,
Enjoy a perfect fit,
Life is complete.

The Essence of Defiance

Into a glass of silence
I poured a luscious wine,
The essence of defiance
Lives in this soul of mine.

The sun sows all the seeds,
They flank on my path,
From innocence of weeds
Into the sea of wrath;
While saintly sinners preach
One foot on the gas pedals,
They later fall into the ditch
Like wilting flowers' petals.

Life saved my fingerprints
As if they were my portraits
Hung in the lifeless labyrinths
Of our banalities and traits.

The swings of moral tourniquets
Don't let even the moneyed in;
While the timeworn etiquettes
Still let them ride in a limousine.

Accustomed to a heavy weight
Of recently acquired frustrations,
My flesh is trembling at the gate
Into the sacred heavenly creations.

Wisdom is Always Blind

Wisdom is always blind,
Like a sclerotic maven:
A harbor for my mind,
A hidden, quiet haven,
A playfield for the wild
Yet intellectual lovechild.

Surprising rite of spring
Awakened curly streams;
The birds relearned to fly.
An old swan starts to sing,
I cry and kiss my dreams
Goodbye.

Although the clouds hover
And disobey their master
Like vultures at the end.
I lost my nature as a lover,
In spite of this disaster,
I gained a loyal friend.

It is our predicting sun,
My blind wisdom gone

The Next Spring's Lovers

I wander through my doubts,
I fly away from the well-known,
Above the labyrinths of crowds,
I seek a gateway to the unknown.

I touch the navel of my universe,
I carve your fables into my verse,
I hold a great mosaic of the arts,
A cradle of your shattered hearts.

The stars fall on my shoulders,
Spark my poetic modest pearls,
Over the unknown paths to walk,
Above the known bridge to burn;
I am dubbed a red-tailed hawk,
The honor I have yet to earn.

I often swim against a current,
I cannot stop; I need to learn it.
I bent the arches of rainbows
My pardon drowned in the flow.
No guilt, no praise, no flowers,
The red-tailed hawk still hovers;
No crimes, no one to blame,
We are the next spring's lovers
Filled with the passion flame.

The Moon Hangs on the Sky

The moon hangs on the sky,
The stars blink with remorse,
At night, the birds don't fly
Above the sleeping shores.

My hair flirts with the gray,
The color of a stormy bay.

The ships sleep in a harbor,
They weren't' t built for that,
I have to dock them farther,
Their boredom is a threat.

I'll never be a wingless worm,
I am a seagull; I love a storm.

A weeping willow idly sways,
Dips branches in the pond,
Only the tides and waves
See sunsets and beyond.

The clouds echoing my songs,
Rain pours its piercing prongs.

Old sailors fold their sails,
Short days or so it seems;
The tunes of nightingales
Fly to the sea of dreams.

My life of lights and fires
Sunk in my dark desires.

The Ocean Gulped the Moon

The ocean gulped the moon,
And tenderly erased the gray;
The tides deleted our gloom,
And set alight the face of day.

We are lying on the silky sheets
Wrinkled by our passion treats;
The twigs of a weeping willow
Cast shaky shadows on the pillow.

You brought to our naughty bed
A silver tray with juice and eggs;
You smile, your cheeks are red,
But I see nothing but your legs.

The scent of lilac filled the room,
I knew our love was at its prime,
If I would only touch the gloom,
I would have stopped the time
Or kiss the lips of death,
And sense your breath;
Then kiss the lips of life,
And catch a falling knife.

Dear Ocean, send back the moon,
Dear moon, bring black and gray,
Dear waves, roll back the gloom.
Long live the sadness of the day.

The Piano of My Soul

The bells will always ring,
The birds of prey or doves
Will always play and sing
The tunes of endless loves.

I play the piano of my soul,
Meanwhile, its shiny wing
Reflects the concert bowl
With melodies of spring.

Love doesn't scare,
A breakup does.
Is it the end of our affair?
Is love a shattered vase?

Is life a blindfolded guillotine?
A watchdog night and day?
Life is somewhere in-between.
Enough-- it is our time to play.

You play; I watch your face:
The plumes of music rush
Into the ecstasy of blaze,
Into your childlike blush.

We sealed forever
The sacred envelope
With our undying fervor,
With our love and hope.

The bells will always ring,
The birds of prey or doves
Will always play and sing
The tunes of endless loves.

The Point of No Return

I lost my priceless twenty years,
I traveled with the Argonauts;
I sailed across the sea of tears
Amid the haves or the have-nots.

I missed the highway to my past,
Rose-tinted glasses hid my tears;
I heard the silence of the blast
And fell into a malady of years.

I walked the bridge into nowhere
Over the point of no return;
I had to cross my Delaware,
The Purple Heart was earned.

I tossed the burden of my lies
And wondered if my turn is close;
I heard the Via Della Rosa sighs,
I am not yet ready for that cross.

I saw the ancient olive trees,
The garden where we prayed,
The place of a famous kiss,
Where Jesus was betrayed,

I saw four vicious fallen angels
That rolled their eyes in rage,
Taking to hell the Holy Grail;
I met four colorful avengers,
That will rewrite our final page,
I guarantee, they never fail.

The Pious Shysters

So-called defenders of the faith
Crawl out of their tight cocoons,
Twisting and turning in the lathe
Of godly truth, under the moons.

Vain and self-righteous
Connoisseurs of truth,
These pious shysters
Brainwash our youth.

The shallow readers
Of the evangelic stuff;
These bottom feeders
Hate that God is love.

The ever-happy Satan grins
He listens to these spinners,
They lie, "We hate the sins,
We love the sinners."

The Storm Performed its Requiem Tonight

The streaks of lightning died in the flight,
The thunders left their echoes at my door;
The storm performed its requiem tonight,
And waits for the well-known tunes to soar.

Dense fog already peeled its blanket,
It is a coffee time; I am not thirsty yet;
A morning dew sparks on my boots
Like gemstones of the pirates' loots.

I crave to circle like a red-tailed hawk
Through Mother Nature's luscious lure:
Across the glowing emeralds of grass,
Over the elegance of autumn's brass,
Above the grandeur of a quiet rapture
Descending onto this endless pasture,
Onto tranquility of a still working clock.
Onto nirvana of a tick-tock, tick-tock…

The Poisons of Betrayals

We make our fancy rounds,
We tease the shiny floors,
The tango's smoky sounds
Take us to foreign shores.

A cheery quilt of our madness
Is just a camouflage of sadness:
The ancient proverbs
Malformed our youth,
We smoked the herbs,
We learned the truth.

We opened curtains
Into the hazy past of sorrows,
Into obscured tomorrows,
Into the masqueraded burdens
That we don't notice anymore,
Nobody ever keeps the score.

The dizzy took it on the chins,
The crazy dumped their sins,
The lackey learned to crawl,
The lucky had a place to fall.

We are the flying darts
Enjoying our sparkly trails,
And heal our wounded hearts
By the dire poisons of betrayals.

Rails of Time

I struggled many years
Before I found my own
Niche,
Before I found my own
Space.
I fought my foes and peers
That led me to the ditch,
And left me in disgrace.

I am surrounded by cynics,
Life is a shooting range.
New songs, old lyrics,
No one will ever change.

We're turning on a dime,
Forsaking our cozy hives;
The shiny rails of our time
Devour trains of our lives.

As sinners we are open-minded,
Eternity is just a fruitless game;
When we are numbed or blinded,
We don't have anyone to blame.

Griefs rocking on the waves,
The river lulls our sorrows,
The birds are mocking
Our yet vacant graves,
While we are dreaming
Of our cloudless tomorrows.

God gives, God often takes,
Nobody shares his or her cakes;
We fight like scorpions in cans,
Thus odors seldom hit the fans.

Psychotic Prophets

We are psychotic prophets
Of our godforsaken lands,
We act like eager moppets
In evil's almighty hands.

We are conductors of ideas,
Mechanics of the minds,
We are presumptuous divas
That blindly lead the blinds.

We fly above the sea of tears,
Between the fights and plays,
From a long comedy of years,
Into a tragedy of happy days.

We turn the fortune's wheels
Against the legal blocks;
And learn the burning thrills
Behind the jailers' locks.

When autumn brings Orion
Into the unsuspicious skies,
Above the scorched horizon,
Above the fiery butterflies,
We watch a carnival of stars
Through prisons' iron bars.

Today, at least, I am free,
No more a hostage of my verse,
I am a priest of glee
Just one of the church's whores.

Rain Washed the Leaves

Rain washed the leaves,
And left behind the griefs
Of autumn's fallen gold.
I knew it is too late to fold.

Life didn't set me free,
Life is an endless siege;
Life gladly tortured me,
Then burned the bridge.

I am injured and betrayed,
But hope, beyond the wall
Sunsets will never fade,
The stars will never fall.

Earth flies the Milky Way
Without aims and goals,
I walk unknown pathways
In search of lonely souls.

I'd rather bark than bite,
Although, I regularly fight.
I haven't been love-bound,
Today, I am a total wreck,
Life calmly turned around
And knifed me in the neck.

Our useless vicious fight
Was dire in every inning.
With my unsteady hand
I signed my will tonight:
Life wasted its beginning,
I didn't waste the end.

From Yesterdays to Hopes

I've chosen my own paths,
Beneath the angels' wraths;
The grandeur of tightropes
From yesterdays to hopes.

My life is a nervous one,
Often deceitful and meager,
Should I just stare at dawn
Or should I pull the trigger?

Once glory-bound
I just annoyed my fate,
And only horsed around
But finally, I wrote a verse;
The critics came too late,
I heard the vultures' curse.

I cut the binding cord,
Then grabbed the bait
Of the unknown world,
I could no longer wait.

It was a requiem for Earth,
A veil of sorrow on its face
Hiding a throbbing birth
Of its integrity and grace.

The sinners die and rise,
Complacency still hovers
Into our vacant paradise,
A golden cage for lovers.

I walk unknown pathways
Across the earthly maze:
The grandeur of tightropes
From yesterdays to hopes.

The Rainy Streams

The rainy streams
Descending from afar,
They look like strings,
The soul of my guitar.

Our goodbye was long
As the incoming train.
I sang my farewell song,
And used the melody of rain.

A rainbow arches in the sky,
Above the foamy puddles,
I hear the bursting bubbles,
And cry. Her eyes are dry.

Her train has left the station,
She thanked me for my song,
It was a genuine appreciation
Of one who used to sing-along.

The long farewell,
The never healing scar.
There is no shepherd
To guide me to her star.

The Rallies Cease

The rallies cease,
The heavens fall,
The theatre of paralysis
Presents its major role
To hungry nouveaux riches,
To greedy moneychangers,
That swim in honey
Like the crafty fish,
But clutch our money
Like the fallen angels.

The innocence of puppeteers
Attempts to camouflage its lies,
I saw no purity in passing years,
Somebody always paid the price.

I didn't waste my youth,
I trailed virginity of truth
Across the world
From dawn to dusk,
From dusk to dawn.
Please, take my word:
The lies have lost their zest
The truths have lost their husk,
I stopped my futile quest:
The comedy and tragedy
Are one.

The Rhythms of Our Hearts

Ideas of the blind
Had reigned
The inconvenience
Of truth;
Our morbid mind
Is tightly chained
To nihilism of youth;
They even brought the arts
Into the beatings of our hearts.

Long way from home,
Tall buildings scratch the skies;
I am a walking metronome,
I give the rhythm to urban cries.

The stage is always lit,
No tremors in my hand,
I have to keep it fit,
I am a drummer of a band;
Our band unites the arts
With rhythms of our hearts.

Hallucinating light,
Anticipation of a wreck,
It is our final night,
Old game; new deck.

There are new cards to play,
No kings, no tens, no aces;
At night, all cats are gray:
Vague silhouettes, no faces;
Life morphs into the arts
The beats of our hearts.

The Road to Damascus

Belle Meade's Starbucks,
A waterhole in Nashville's desert,
Oasis in a concrete labyrinth of time,
Where quiet loners lined like ducks,
Subconsciously attempting to divert
Their timid dullness to a bit sublime.

I watch this game,
While peeping at the youth,
Trying to understand and frame
Old paradigm into a newer truth.

The road to Damascus
Was never walked by me,
Only St. Paul and other rascals
Told me to fight and die or flee.
I want to meet them face to face
I want to be a part of human race:
To shave my thick-necked head
To match the cocky bodyguards,
The good old boys often breastfed
That whistle Dixie past graveyards.

The fortress of my independence
Unquestionably crumbling,
While I am still deftly mumbling,
Impressing owners in attendance.
There is a place for every whore,
Even for slothful gate keepers;
I can't coexist a minute more
Among lackluster weepers,
Among dejected mourners
Daydreaming of a paradise,
But shrewdly cutting corners
Like hockey players on the ice.

There is no pulse in darkness,
Forever cold, forever heartless.
I am on the road to Damascus
Under a star-studded nightly quilt,
I walk the road to Damascus
Along a self-inflicted endless guilt.

The Sacred Key

My Lord, I sinned:
You put the wind
Into my eager sail,
I ran away from jail.

A bad tattoo on my forearm,
A footprint of my sorrows,
The stigma of the harm,
Will shadow my tomorrows.

The power of my rage
Can climb the tallest pole,
But cannot leave the cage
Hosting my tortured soul.

Under the clouds of my visions,
Among the orbits of my worlds,
I draw the lines; I make decisions,
I carve the finest filigree of words.

Look at my daring art,
Enjoy my last creation,
It is the beating heart
Of my imagination.

The midst of night,
The birds don't sing.
It is my final flight,
It is my final spring.

I turn the sacred key,
Open the golden cage,
And let my verses flee
Toward the final page.

The Same Old Route

I didn't excite my fate:
A constant drought,
The same old street,
The same old gate,
The same old route,
The same heartbeat.

I peeled my eyes,
I pulled the drapes,
No tears, no cries,
Just sour grapes.

I'm digging in my heels,
I am thirsty; lips are dry,
I never knew how it feels
To eat and have a pie.

I never try to poke
The rings of smoke
Above the saints;
The evening faints,
Poor little fellows
Enjoy their haloes.

I wear a poker face,
My dog is in the race.
The miles of lies,
The yards of truth,
Some honey for the flies,
Some wounds to soothe,
The real pain is in details,
Let's hear the fairytales:
A silver lining has a cloud,
Maybe the other way about;

Under the rainbow's paints
The sinners love their saints.
The chosen few stir ripples
To irritate inertia in peoples;
The known world explodes
With olden truths and frauds.

I try to tempt my fate,
I am sure it is too late.

The Scent of Mirth

I write my daily log,
Hot, hazy afternoon
With naughty breezes;
At night, my lazy dog
Barks at the moon,
Till summer ceases.

The water streaks
Caress the ferry,
Rain pours for weeks,
Only the lake is merry.

The ripples roll
Toward the fall.
My nimble sailboat
Rocks in its berth,
September brought
The scent of mirth.

The rains can't cease,
I humbly bear and wait
Through my long nights,
Until the autumn breeze,
Intriguing as a lovely date,
Unveils mysterious delights.

Streaming Tunes

The wasted harmony of days,
The nights of a bitter solitude,
I hear the lonely pianist plays
His tempting succulent etude.

The waterfalls of silver moons
Brought fairytales into my soul.
The snowfalls cover the nights,
And streams of endless tunes
Help to rehearse the title role
Beyond the melodies of lights.

I am confused at times,
I like the gloomy moons,
I like the muffled rhymes,
I like enthusiastic tunes.

The Shores of Youth

Over the crumbled bricks
Of our silent yesteryears,
My memory still brings
Some honey to my ears.

The winds of hot September
Dropped apples on the grass;
Those days I still remember,
I used to skip my English class.

My granny keenly loved to bake,
She had a little house on the lake,
She called it manna from the sky
When I'd bring apples for her pie.

The favorite old-fashioned joy,
My granny's tea with apple pie,
It was a real heaven for a boy,
To be there, I didn't have to fly.

I treasure these romantic treats
From the fading shores of youth,
Years pass yet history repeats
Often to hurt, seldom to soothe.

Leviathan Was Just a River Pike

Bold faces wearing nylon wigs
Still crave their mothers' nipples;
Deep-rooted etiquettes reversed,
Only the lawyers are well versed.
If that's the promised paradise,
I'd rather keep my hellish glee
Under a weeping willow's twigs
Caressing ponds without ripples.

My soul is dark; my pain is dire
And needs a spark to set a fire,
It needs to feel the heat of Hell,
Don't worry; I am doing well.

I want the truth of deaths revealed,
I see a grave; I want to get inside,
I am too old, I have no time to yield,
While cities turn into a countryside,
Where all the wordless talk,
Where all the legless walk,
Where no one ever works,
Where mothers hate the storks.

The Christians destroyed my verses,
The Jews just panned and laughed,
The Muslims simply raised a sword.
Only a hidden stairway to paradise,
Only the four apocalyptic horses,
And Solomon's poor baby halved,
May save our disintegrating world.

I hit the wall; it was a lucky strike,
Here's a final chapter of my book:

Leviathan was just a river pike,
I let that "monster" off the hook.

I scrutinized the Devil's eyes
Right under the Wisdom tree,
And realized: if this is paradise,
I'd rather have the Hell as glee.

Regrettably, I Lost …

My heartless unfilled chest,
A skeleton of freezing cage,
A carcass of a dead house,
My timid tombstone stands
As a sad symbol of despair.
The mad-caps do their best
With their pretentious rage;
I hear profanity-laced rants
Of every high-pitched louse,
A noise I can no longer bear.

My life is a gigantic question
Minus the necessary answer;
My views are never innocent,
Irony is a learned profession;
My wit is a malignant cancer
Sending an awful fishy scent.

A dark and murky yesterday
Fused with a bright tomorrow,
Delivers birth of a dull today.
My tortured, weary heart
Draped in a quilt of sorrow
Lies on a butcher's tray
And craves a life to start.
I didn't choose to hibernate,
My life is hanging on a hair
I'd never passionately wait
For my foretold nightmare.

Fresh chill of winter snows,
A loud echo of spring rains,
Foresaw the autumn glows,
Predicted brutal hurricanes.

I sadly watched a hectic fall
Of my dog-tired yellow pages
Wearily remembering my life;
Then I received a tempting call
And jumped into the pit of ages.
Regrettably, I lost my final strife.

The Last Teardrop

The nightmares of my night,
The fervor of the crowds,
The blues of rumbling skies,
The leaded thunderclouds
Obscured the blinding light
Of our convoluted lies.

I wiped the last teardrop.
The angels of my sky
Will bring the spring,
The wars will stop,
The mothers will not cry,
The birds will sing,

I try to rise above
My gloomy ceiling
And face the world;
The world of love,
The world of healing,
Not of a risen sword.

I mean
Only the dead
Have seen
The happy end.

Epigraph

Unknown Pathways are the avenues of our dreams.
PZ

Acknowledgements

I am deeply grateful to Judith Broadbent
For her skilled professional guidance
And generous stewardship;
For her unyielding yet wise editing,
Which allows me enough room
To exercise my whims.

To Anna Dikalova for her kind ideas
and a firm belief in my success.

To a great artist, Mary Anne Capeci,
who graciously allowed me to use
her painting for the cover of this book.

To all my friends for their continuous
And gently expressed motivations.

Thank y'all, PZ

Printed in the United States
By Bookmasters